MW01251169

# Conscious Unparenting™

## Our 1970's Spin on Modern-Day Motherhood

### By Kim Kinzie
### and
### Dawn Michael

This book is non-fiction. Certain names and identifying details have been changed in order to protect the privacy of individuals involved.

Two '70s Moms Publishing
East Greenwich, RI
USA

Copyright © Kim Kinzie and Dawn Michael

ALL RIGHTS RESERVED. No part of this book may be reproduced, scanned or distributed in any printed or electric form without express permission in writing from the publisher. Please do not participate in or encourage piracy of copyrighted materials in violation of the Authors' rights. Purchase only authorized editions.

Edited by Solidus Editorial Solutions
COVER DESIGN: JANSEN MAE TONGCO
AUTHOR PHOTO: JILLIAN BODOFF

ISBN 978-0-9864398-0-3

Library of Congress Control Number: 2015901043

For more information about the authors and their mission, please visit *www.consciousunparenting.com*.

This book is dedicated to our moms, who made motherhood look easy, and to our children, who proved the opposite.

# TABLE OF CONTENTS

Acknowledgements .................................................................5

Preface ..............................................................................7

Introduction........................................................................ 11

I.    If Boredom is the Mother of Invention,
      Then Call Me Thomas Edison. ...................................... 17

II.   How Did a Golden Retriever End Up With
      Three Chocolate Labs? .................................................29

III.  The Ring Test Failed Me...............................................39

IV.   You Call This a Vacation???...........................................49

V.    Rocket Science is for Wimps. .......................................59

VI.   My Husband's Girlfriend. .............................................69

VII.  You're Going to Miss These Days!.................................77

VIII. Fifty Shades of Black and White,
      But Definitely Not Gray. ..............................................87

IX.   Forget the College Fund and Save for Therapy. ...........95

X.    Choose Wisely.............................................................101

CONCLUSION ..............................................................109

ABOUT THE AUTHORS ..............................................121

# Acknowledgements

When we first talked about writing a book together, we thought we would interview other women and tell their stories. We spent many months (and a fair amount of money) drinking with and talking to friends, family, co-workers, neighbors and even some strangers.

While we heard some amazing tales and gathered invaluable information, we felt ill-equipped to tell other people's stories; instead we opted for embarrassing ourselves. Nonetheless, we want to acknowledge all the incredible women we spoke with and thank them, profusely, for their honesty. Hearing their truths has changed us as women and mothers, and for that we are eternally grateful. Here they are: Jane A'Hearn, Karli Grant Argus, Jaclyn Bova, Anne Bradley, Kristen Cody, Elizabeth Fernald, Stacey Gorbachev, Christine Nardelli Harding, Cheryl Kendra, Amy Larson, Jen Martino, Rhonda Maggiacomo, Tammy McDevitt, Kathy Michael, Michelle Meegan, Sherry Morra, Gretchen Phillips, Patty Pollock, Kelly Rivera and Elisa Sullivan.

To those women (and man) who read our numerous drafts, and provided us with honest, thoughtful feedback: Jill Bodoff, Lynne Chevoya, Deb McGann Dilts, Mark Fogarty, Debbie Kiley, Anna Lesczynski, Deb Lundin, Emily Olson, Nancy Olson,

Stephanie O'Rourke, Alexandra Penn-Bibb, Jane Regnante, Susy Reyes, and Christine Welch.

To the many other people who provided us with much support and friendship; who, when we told them we were writing a book, didn't roll their eyes or try to dissuade us. You gave us writing and publishing advice and watched our kids so we could meet for countless editing lunches. There are too many of you to name here, but we want to pay special thanks to those of you who, but for, we might not ever have completed this book: Christine Collins, Hulya D'Arrigo, Karen Danielson Engeian, Stefanie Pontifice Head, Chrissi "Creepy Crawley" Howell, Chris Jarvis, Andy and Judy Kinzie, Jessica Kinzie, Micaela Materne, Jim and Marilyn O'Shea, Charlene Schlect, Elisabeth Shenanga, and Dawn Stricker.

A special thank you to Sara Weintraub and Designs by Gary for helping us bring our disco ball idea to life, and to Jill Bodoff (again) for your incredible photography skills.

Finally, to our husbands and children: thanks for giving us the inspiration to write this book, as well as the material to fill its pages. More importantly, thank you for allowing us to share these stories. We couldn't have accomplished this dream without your love and support.

# PREFACE

*Who are we and why are we writing this book?*

*We are lifelong friends who met in fifth grade, when Dawn had the misfortune of being the new kid. She further had the misfortune of being extraordinarily tall and dorky, adorned with braces and large-framed glasses that bore her initials in the bottom corner of the lens...in gold. Needless to say she had a tough time fitting in. Kim suffered from a similar fate, but only because she was on the cusp of being cool, as opposed to actually being cool. So to fit in, she did many things she otherwise would never had considered doing: feigned a love for the band KISS, wore only t-shirts and corduroys... and assisted in relentlessly teasing the new kids. The reader should therefore not be surprised to learn that Kim and Dawn did not become immediate friends.*

*Fast-forward a few years to high school. Dawn's looks have vastly improved but her nerd status persisted. She joined such rebellious groups as Students Against Drunk Driving, the math club and the high school band, in which she played clarinet. It's important to note here that these events took place in the 1980s, well before* Glee *and therefore well before the time when playing in the high school band provided you with any cache. Dawn studied hard and made good friends, all of whom were equally nerdy.*

*Kim followed a different path in high school. She too had a desire to succeed, but was not really interested in studying hard to achieve that dream. Instead she was interested in trying new things: sex, alcohol and breaking the record for most school days missed while still managing to graduate (for those of you who are curious, the answer is forty-five. Be forewarned: you will need to make up some gym classes).*

*Fatefully Kim and Dawn both ended up working after school at a small market in their hometown, one known for its fruit baskets, quality meats and other attributes that cannot be mentioned here for fear of civil and/or criminal liability. Kim and Dawn ran the cash registers together, and, in between scanning, bagging and collecting cash, became fast friends.*

*We are very different people. Dawn has a kind, sweet, gentle personality and likes to avoid confrontation at all costs. She has an affinity for the ballet, theater and designer handbags. Kim, on the other hand, loves vampires, bacon and Jon Stewart, and doesn't shy away from a good fight. Despite these differences, we've always learned from one another. We are the self-proclaimed yin to one another's yang, and it's always served us well.*

*Now here we are, middle-aged moms who are completely disenchanted with this banal existence called motherhood. Having always had a shared passion for the written word, together we set out to write a book. Our dream was not to simply write a tome in which we complain about the woes of motherhood; instead we wanted to create change, to make parenting more tolerable -- possibly even enjoyable.*

*We started the process by interviewing other women to determine if we were the only ones who felt similarly disenchanted. Although we've read countless books and blog entries on the subject, we needed to know how the women in our everyday lives felt. Those we met at PTA meetings or kids' birthday parties seemed to have this mothering thing perfected. They managed to exercise, look coiffed and talk about their children with only love and admiration. How would they react if they heard our stories?*

*We decided the best way to answer that question would be to simply ask them. So we approached our close friends and other women in our lives and invited them to take part in an honest discussion on motherhood. We called these sessions "focus groups," even if they felt like mere excuses to get away from our families for a bit. Either way, the process was revealing — it's amazing what happens when you open up to people and ask them to do the same. The women we spoke to unexpectedly told us things we'd never heard before, even from our closest friends. Their stories were hilarious, heartfelt, raw, intense — in other words, they were just like our stories. Better yet, they weren't horrified by what we had to say.*

*From these gatherings we made two important discoveries. First, despite appearances, many other women feel like we do about parenting. Second, being in the company of authentic women is a key ingredient to happier parenting. These discoveries, along with our stories, provided the inspiration for this book. We hope you feel similarly inspired to institute the changes necessary for a more fulfilling motherhood experience.*

# INTRODUCTION

As much as we like to pretend we're eternally in our 20s, we're not. As a matter of fact, we're so old that, had we done things differently, we could be grandparents by now. We are children of the 1970s who lived in the era of eight-tracks, *Creature Double Feature* and riding in the "way-back" of the station wagon while our moms puffed on their Virginia Slims, windows buttoned up to ensure we received plenty of second-hand smoke.

We also lived during a time when motherhood looked much more effortless. Many moms of the '70s look at us modern parents, shrug their shoulders and say, "What's all the fuss? In our day, we just did it."

It's true. They didn't buy cookbooks that taught them creative ways to hide vegetables in cake; they just made us eat our vegetables – they were in control. Better yet, they didn't care what we ate, as they happily threw a TV dinner in the oven or heated up a can of ravioli. Either way, our parents didn't overanalyze every decision, but instead unwittingly relied on their own experience and intuition. In their words, they "just did it."

Unlike those laid-back parents of the 1970s, our lives revolve around our children. We obsess over all aspects of their young lives. With constant conversations about childhood obesity and diabetes, we worry about everything they eat and drink. We fret that they're having too much screen-time and not enough exercise. As they get older, we are told to monitor their online activities to make sure they're not being cyber-bullied or sexting naked selfies to the football team. We put ourselves thousands of dollars into debt to ensure a good, solid education for our children.

To hone our parenting skills, we read endless books and articles that teach us about positive discipline – to be "firm but kind." We are told the importance of developing our children's emotional intelligence and helping them to manage their anger. Meanwhile, we're all human pressure cookers, ready to blow at a moment's notice, screaming at our kids: "WE DON'T YELL AT EACH OTHER WHEN WE'RE MAD! WE USE KIND WORDS!" What a joke!

We foolishly thought parenting would be like it was for our mothers, or at least something like that. Even still, we did our homework. We read books, asked others for their thoughts and opinions, and watched our friends have babies. Never did the truth reveal itself: modern-day parenting is the emotional, physical and psychological challenge of a lifetime.

Did everyone lie? Did we ask the wrong people? Did our friends intentionally alter reality, presenting only a façade of happiness and joy? Or were they being honest and we're the crazy, incompetent fools who simply can't handle parenting?

Admittedly, people told us that having kids would change our lives; it would be hard, but the rewards would make it all worthwhile. Statements like those are innocuous and, quite frankly, not much help. They are statements more apropos for someone who's contemplating, say, a triathlon or graduate school. In both scenarios, if you don't like it, you have an out. Parenting – once you're in, you're in for life. Such a decision really deserves the truth – a realistic assessment of the day-to-day grind. We got nothing of the sort.

So here were are – the misled and somewhat clueless moms who love our kids but don't love motherhood. There, we said it. We don't love motherhood. We know how lucky we are to have healthy, happy, wonderful children. We realize we are so fortunate to be raising kids in our comfortable, middle-class existence. We really have nothing to complain about, but yet here we are – grumbling nonetheless.

We often wish we could parent like they did in the '70s – a bit more relaxed without all the fuss. We're not suggesting those days were preferable. They weren't the halcyon days, by any stretch. After all, it's not long after Diazepam (Valium) was brought to the market, and given the nickname "Mother's Little Helper."

Also, their laid-back approach to parenting now appears somewhat impulsive and hasty, making our parents the easy scapegoat for the issues we face in adulthood. Most of us were spanked, perhaps even victims of the dreaded belt. Some of us were latchkey kids - at the tender age of eight or nine - waiting in the garage for mom to come home from work because we were too frightened to enter the house alone. We were left with sitters every Saturday night, and sometimes for a week or two at a time while our parents went on vacation without us. Oh, the damage those reckless actions must have caused!

In our attempt to right what we now perceive to be their wrongs, we've gone to the other extreme. We've created the monster known as modern-day parenthood – the relentless, demanding, less-than-truthful way in which many of us raise our children in the 21st century.

Modern-day parents expect themselves to be perfect in every way. We've instituted these self-imposed directives to make our child the best: the best student, the best athlete, the most charitable, the kindest person. We strive to make ourselves the best parent possible: world-class organic chef, playmate extraordinaire, creator of magical summer vacations. While these goals all seem honorable, what's the cost to us parents? More importantly, what's the cost to our kids?

This pressure to give your child the best of everything and be their world protector has created the infamous "helicopter parent." You know you're in their presence when you hear the "thwack, thwack, thwack" of helicopter blades as they monitor their child's every movement and involve themselves in all aspect's of their kids' lives – how exhausting!

Those who try to parent in a more relaxed manner find their own challenges. They notice they're the only ones in their social circle who are so lackadaisical. Other parents look at them with scorn. They hear on the news that parents who do things they do (like leave their kids in the car while they run into the dry cleaners) are getting arrested.

No matter which route you choose, you never feel like you're good enough. That's the joy of modern-day-parenting.

This lifestyle is not sustainable. As you'll see from our stories, we embody a "different" sort of parenting: one that's more relaxed and less guilt-ridden, one that mixes the best of the '70s with the best of today. Taking a cue from Gwyneth Paltrow and Chris Martin's "conscious uncoupling," we are calling this philosophy "conscious unparenting™" – intentionally taking a step back from hyper-parenting and diverting that freed-up energy to attending to your own needs.

To embrace this mindset, you don't need to become a pretentious vegan and name your kids after a prophet and a piece of fruit. And, we're not talking about checking out of parenthood, existing only in the three-martini play date. That would be more fittingly called "unconscious parenting." Instead we're talking about having a more balanced approach so that you become important and your needs stand alongside those of your children, as opposed to well behind them. It means truly giving up the guilt, knowing that you're doing your best, even if your best looks pretty frightening at times.

We know this might not be easy. You'll need to find friends with whom you share this new mode of parenting. As we mentioned in the preface, one surprising consequence of those focus groups was the realization that we *need* -- not just want -- to be in the company of other women.

Why is this so surprising? For years we've been hearing, "It takes a village to raise a child." We never gave the saying much thought, as it seemed more applicable to life before the Industrial Revolution or worse, living on a commune. We'll keep our HBO and appliances, and skip the Kool-Aid, thank you very much. As the parenting years have ticked by, however, the true meaning of the saying has become clear: We women-folk need each other. We don't just need help with carpools and hand-me-downs; we need a safe harbor, a person to whom we can say anything and know it will be received without judgment.

Unfortunately men cannot fulfill this role for us. Even those of us with the most supportive partners understand the issue: men need to fix problems. When they hear us gripe about our kids or housework, they must find a solution, even if we don't want one. Women, on the other hand, know the power of a good bitch session. Nothing beats having a village of women to whom you can kvetch.

One of our goals is to help each woman find that village. You might have noticed the book cover displays a shiny disco ball.

We strive to make this the symbol for a more relaxed, friendly mode of parenting. We chose a disco ball because it's the ultimate '70s icon, a reminder to have fun, feel carefree, do "The Hustle." The gay movement has the rainbow; the hippies have their peace sign. Why can't we have our disco ball? We'll talk more in the conclusion about how we can use this symbol to connect with one another and start a conscious unparenting™ movement.

We realize this book won't appeal to everyone. Many will find our stories offensive; some might disagree with our philosophy. But some of you might applaud our honesty. Many of you might think, "Finally, someone is saying what I've been feeling for years!" Some of you might find comfort in knowing you're not alone and realizing there's hope that motherhood will get easier and more enjoyable.

Be forewarned that this book, like parenthood, is a bit of a roller coaster ride – one minute you're laughing, the next minute you're crying. You hope this ride never ends, then you can't wait to get off. The tone is light and happy, then it moves to dark and more serious.

Also, please know that we won't spend much time gushing about how much we love our children. Of course we love them, but that's the easy part; it's parenting them that's hard. Many books and stories we've read about the challenges of motherhood have a happy ending in which the author, recalling the smell of her daughter's hair or the sight of her son's smile, realizes it's all worth it. Our book too has a happy ending, but it's more about changing the demands of modern day parenthood. Some days those memories or sensory perceptions just aren't enough.

If you think this mindset is for you, please read on. By the end you might just find yourself starting a parenting revolution. But first, here are the stories that started it all ...

# I. If Boredom is the Mother of Invention, Then Call Me Thomas Edison.

*By Kim*

Parenting young children can be so dreadfully boring; something I did not expect. I guessed it would be challenging, exhausting, and messy. I just never anticipated this level of ennui. I often wonder: Is it me, or is it them?

I recently discussed this fact with a friend who had the good sense not to have kids. (I mean, the poor thing who missed out on this amazing experience). Anyway, she looked me square in the eye and said, "It's not supposed to be fun. It's your job."

How true. I guess I just chose a fairly boring job, which is ironic because that's something I scrupulously avoided before having children. I'm a lawyer and began my legal career as a prosecutor, not because I had some altruistic need to put criminals behind bars, but because being in court every day was FUN. I loved the back and forth with defense attorneys, drinking coffee with the cops, running from courtroom to courtroom with an armload of files. Every day felt like a new, exciting adventure. The day they gave me a promotion and stuck me at a desk to prepare the more serious cases, I started to love it less and eventually quit to pursue something, you guessed it, more fun.

Never having found a job more stimulating than my first gig as a prosecutor, I decided to give up the law and stay home with my brood. Did I expect it to be fun? I truthfully can't recall. Even still, I understand that not everything worth doing is fun; sometimes it's honorable, or satisfying, or the right thing to do – and that is enough. Are proctologists having fun at their jobs? I highly doubt it, yet I'm grateful for their work. Nonetheless, does parenting have to be so mind numbing?

Admittedly, before having children I thought parenting looked rather dreadful. Spending every weekend at a soccer field or watching a play about broccoli and eggplant was not my idea of a good time. I expressed this sentiment to many people and always received the same response: "When it's your own child, you'll feel differently." Phew.

When my son was born I did spend hours upon hours staring at his gorgeous face and never felt a tinge of boredom. Jump ahead a month or two, when baby is awake several hours of the day and face-gazing occupies only a few minutes' time. Enter boredom.

Unsure what to do with my baby, I turned to the parenting books, which all suggested various forms of infant play: hand him blocks, hold a mirror in front of his face, shake a rattle, etc. While these suggestions were helpful, they took a mere ten, fifteen minutes. What does one do with the other seven hours and fifty minutes of the day that baby is awake? I tried putting him on his expensive, colorful play mat, or in his even more costly (but useless) swing, but he only wanted to be held. Next I tried the sling. This worked beautifully for a walk around the neighborhood or bringing him to a party, but what about at home? Despite what the accompanying DVD led me to believe, I couldn't wash dishes or write emails while wearing my sling. I remember simply walking around the house, pointing out pictures on the wall, appliances, towels and similar thrilling household items to "connect my baby with his home," as one parenting book suggested. Truthfully I felt like a boob as I cheerfully showed him the dryer, desperate for something to do.

Getting out of the house helped. I eventually joined a play-group and met a group of moms with whom I spent my mornings. I couldn't wait to meet them for a walk, a picnic, a root canal – anything to have companionship. I began to enjoy motherhood. As the months ticked by, however, my boredom resurfaced as my son dropped to one nap. My fellow moms now spent their afternoons at home, having a respite while their babies took a two-, three- or sometimes four-hour nap. My son, however, never napped for more than forty-five minutes at a time. My afternoons were therefore dreadfully long.

Unsure what to do with all this free time, I got on the floor and played with him. Sadly I found my mind drifting after a mere minute or two, yearning to check my email or turn on the TV and watch a *Law and Order* rerun: *SVU*, *Criminal Intent*, even *Trial by Jury* – anything but another minute of play.

He whined or cried when I tried to get on my computer or phone, so I cleaned the house, a lot. I started baking, often. I did these activities because my son seemed very content to watch me cook or clean – must be the testosterone. I've never been so bored (and fat, and tidy) in my entire life. No one else at playgroup mentioned this problem so I guessed it was just me – me and my non-napping child.

At some point we decided to have another baby. Why? I'm still not sure. Jump ahead two years because quite frankly those first years of life with two young children is just a blur. I am now the mom of two active young boys and my boredom level has reached epic proportions. At this point you might be saying to yourself, "Oh woman, please – just get out of the house and go for a walk." I do go for walks; as a matter of fact, I'm typically out of my house by nine each morning, engaging in some kid-friendly activity. The problem, however, is the fact that I'm doing these activities alone. We recently moved our family from San Diego to our native Rhode Island and I therefore have had to rebuild my mom community. It's taken longer than expected, so most days it's just my kids and me. For me, this is tantamount to waterboarding.

Take today, for example. I brought my boys to an indoor gym. They love it there and are so happy to jump on trampolines or push around large, soft rollers. They have an absolute blast, but like every other activity in our repertoire, it's all about them. I keep asking myself, "Can't someone who works here watch my kids so I can go do an errand or read a book?" Alas, no. They require you to be within arm's reach of your children at all times. Have you ever tried being within arm's reach of two boys who are not Siamese twins? Impossible.

As I stand there playing sentry, I scan the crowd looking for someone nice with whom I can strike up a conversation. Instead I see women who are already coupled up, or worse, moms who are playing ball with their children or joining them on the balance beam. Are these women accessing their inner child and truly enjoying this play? Or are they sociopaths whose sole purpose in life is to make other moms look insufficient?

Later that afternoon while the kids were having their TV time, I went online and read a blog post written, in the form of an open letter, to a mom on her cell phone at an indoor play place.[1] What a coincidence, I thought, as I'd spent the day at a play place, and did turn to my cell phone occasionally to check email or play a quick game of Free Cell. I'd hoped the author

---

1    *An Open Letter to the Mom on Her Cell Phone @ the Playplace*, http://christinasbooks.com/blog, (September 23, 2010)

would give the mom a pass, acknowledging how dull it is to otherwise sit alone at an indoor play place. Instead, she chastised the mom, who apparently sat fixated on her cell phone while her child played alone, shooting other kids with an imaginary gun. The author went on to say that, if you get in the habit of being on your phone, your kids will get in the habit of being ignored. The end result: your kid becomes a brat.

Great. Fears confirmed: I'm a shitty mother because I'm bored, and I'm turning my children into brats. But then I thought about the moms who went with a friend. They weren't giving their kids attention; they were chatting while their kids played. Are they too creating brats? Why is it okay to ignore your child if you're having a face-to-face conversation, but not an electronic one?

It was then I realized – it's all bullshit. Ignoring your child at a play place designed exclusively for children is perfectly fine – no matter the distraction. Why? First of all, you're there so someone or something other than you can entertain your children. Your participation is not required; it's why you paid the ten dollar entry fee. Also, you've watched your children jump on a trampoline or throw a ball hundreds, if not thousands of times. Why must you watch it again?

This is especially true for the playground. I lived in San Diego for the first five years of my older son's life, where the year-round perfect weather allowed me to bring him to a playground four to five times each week. The first few times I pushed him on the swing, I did relish that look of glee on his face. I snapped a few photos, probably even took a video. The eighty-second time, however, I was either chatting away with a friend or on my cell phone. What the hell else am I expected to do? Smile at him the entire time and pretend I'm entranced by that same old look of glee on his face? I'm not. I've seen it many times. It hasn't changed. I have photos.

Maybe the experience would be different if I suffered from short-term memory loss, like Drew Barrymore in that movie *50 First Dates*, where each day she wakes up not remembering her past. Her boyfriend, Adam Sandler, must convince her that they're in love by engineering a perfect date – every day. If I were like Drew, I could go to the playground and relish watching my child go down the slide, again. Instead, however, I'm in the Adam Sandler role, repeating myself day in and day out, dutifully pretending that it feels like the first time, every time.

Endless repetition isn't fun for anyone – even Adam Sandler got frustrated– and when you're a parent (particularly one who stays home), repetition rules the day. I've done it all and I'm over it. I don't really enjoy getting on the floor and playing with my children. At their current ages (five and two), I have found a few activities I don't find terribly torturous like drawing or playing Hide and Seek. (I always make sure to hide really well. Did you know one can cat-nap in a closet?). We read books and do lots of snuggling – that stuff I love. They also assist me in the kitchen and are becoming avid little bakers – must be from all those days watching me do the baking. Other than that, though, I'm out.

Some of you modern-day moms might hate me at this point. You might be asking, "Why did you have kids in the first place?" Good question. One I ask myself some days. Then I think about my childhood. As a child of the '70s and '80s, I lived outdoors, like all the kids in my neighborhood. Our parents threw us out in the morning and we stayed outside with our friends until we were called in for a meal. The weather was irrelevant – we were outside. The memories I made on my own were some of my happiest: riding bikes for hours on end with my best friend

Karen; building snow forts in the winter; making mud pies in the spring. We explored our contained world and made up crazy games like "The Russians Are Coming" (we didn't know about Al Qaeda in those days). My parents' absence from those memories is not something I mourn but rather celebrate, as I felt my first hints of independence.

I recently read a *Boston Globe* article titled "Leave Those Kids Alone,"[2] which speaks to this very issue. The author stated that, though it's important to interact with our children, we don't need to get on the floor and play with them. Not only is it unnecessary, it's unnatural. This article is like my bible, as it validates my belief in neglect. I clutch it as though it were a lost commandment: "Thou shalt not extensively play with thy children" – now there's one to which I can abide. I confidently say "You can play that by yourself" with each tortured request of "Mommy, play train tracks" or "You be the Mommy Cheetah and I'll be the baby Cheetah." No can do, son. Don't want to mess with the experts and/or Moses.

So here I am, the mom of two children with whom I rarely play. I am able to resume my domestic role as housekeeper and cook. In between scrubbing toilets and preparing dinner, I desperately search for a quick fix of entertainment. Where do I go? Why, Facebook, of course.

Facebook is not a place to go when you're feeling even remotely insecure about your parenting abilities. And despite my reliance on the no-play commandment, I often feel guilty about my neglectful ways, my yelling and many other bad parenting acts I bestow upon my children on a daily basis. But there I went,

2    Christopher Shea, *Leave Those kids Alone: The Idea That Adults Should Be Playing With Their Kids Is a Modern Invention – and Not Necessarily a Good One*, Boston Globe, (July 15, 2007).

because my only other option was Pinterest, and if you think Facebook makes you feel like a loser, Pinterest will have you joining the Anthony Michael Hall group from a John Hughes film.

One day as I moved from a friend's profile, to that of a friend of friend, I asked myself "What am I doing here? I don't even know this person!" I didn't care because it was something to do, so I continued. Being a stay-at-home mom like myself, I thought she might provide some interesting quips and I could bond with a stranger. She listed her position as CEO of Justin, Sarah and Aaron Corporation, presumably the names of her children. This is sort of a cute statement for a stay-at-home mom so it didn't annoy me until I saw her description of the job: "Best job I've ever had and I love my bosses!"

Now wait a minute. First of all, if she is CEO, why are the kids her bosses? What kind of parent calls her toddler "the boss?" In my house, I'm the boss. Even if this is not true in reality, you bet your ass it's what my kids think. Second of all, what kind of person thinks that staying at home with small children is the best job ever? Clearly her prior occupations must have been horribly dreadful, possibly the cleaner of Porta Potties, the janitor of a triple-X theater or a podiatrist.

I scanned her wall, which she conveniently did not make private and noted that she posted almost daily, typically talking about her children's accomplishments: karate belts attained, soccer goals scored, spelling bees won (or merely participated in … does it really matter? She has a photo and she's going to use it). She gushed about their adorable antics: "Today Aaron told me that I was the best mommy ever; even better than Caillou's mom. Boy do I feel blessed!" Oh yes, you are so blessed, Miss Stranger. How wonderful that you fare better than the mom of a whiny cartoon character who is inexplicably bald at the age of four. Why is a comment like this on Facebook? More importantly, if parenting is so exciting and wonderful, why is she spending so much time on Facebook at all? She's here because she's bored; she just doesn't have the balls to admit it. Why is being bored so controversial? It's nothing new. Our parents, while not playing with us, were smoking cigarettes and watching soaps, right?

I now understand all those sitcoms where the woman is counting down the minutes until her spouse gets home so she can shove the kids in his arms and have an escape. For me, though, it's more about the company. I just want to talk to an adult. I pine for the weekends and fantasize about taking the kids to the park for a picnic or out to dinner. I'm realistic so I picture us at Applebee's or Chili's. I imagine me sitting in the red pleather booth, salted margarita in hand, having an actual conversation with my husband while the kids color in their menus. When reality hits, however, taking our children to a restaurant is about as much fun as a colonoscopy. Actually, I've had a colonoscopy and I think I'd endure another one over a night at Applebee's with my two-year-old. The park is more of the same, except now my husband also must feign excitement at our children's look of glee on the swing. Yawn.

Of course we do some fun things together, but they're only mildly fun. Most weekends my husband and I sit around sort of staring at each other, mystified as to what to do, looking at the clock and asking "Is it time to put them to bed yet?" I can see the joy in his face as Sunday night approaches, because tomorrow he'll be in the land of grown-ups. He won't have to discipline or break up fights or watch his swear words. He loves going back to work and I envy the motherfucker more than he'll ever know.

On one of these Sunday evenings I asked my husband, just out of curiosity, how he felt about being a parent. He gave me the generic answer, "I love my kids."

"Yeah, yeah, but how do you feel about *parenting*? I ask because I've noticed that for me, my most enjoyable parenting moments have been when we are with other people who have children. Our kids are playing happily with their kids and I have an alcoholic drink of some kind in my hand. Is that wrong?"

This seemed a sad statement, the saddest part being that he agreed with me. We further agreed that we even preferred hanging around with boring adults to being stuck in the house with our kids. What did this say about us as parents?

I'm happy to say that, as my older son approaches the age of six, I am beginning to see a light at the end of this boredom tunnel. He has a unique sense of humor and we actually sit and talk. There exists a long list of activities that we can do together that we *both* enjoy. It's not all about me, but it's no longer all about him. It's about *us*, which is a nice change. I even enjoy watching him "act" in plays with no storyline. (The soccer, however, has already passed the "boredom due to repetition" threshold.) The future, too, looks bright as there are many things I look forward to doing together: reading *Harry Potter*, seeing scary movies, going for long bike rides, braving roller coasters, taking day trips to New York City – a chance to show him all the things I love about the world, and watch him shower me with appreciation.

The irony is that, the more interesting he gets, the less interesting I will most likely become to him. I am beginning to understand now why people continue to breed – always looking for that sweet spot when you and your child are equally interested in one another. Or maybe not everyone finds babies and toddlers as boring as I do. I suppose you're the same people who love a good performance of *The Nutcracker* or who found *The English Patient* to be a riveting film.

Am I a bad mother? I highly doubt it, even though I do feel the guilt creep back in whenever I see Facebook photos of parents doing major craft projects with their kids or playing endless games of Candy Land. Then I think about what it truly means to be a parent. Parenting is not reserved for those people who enjoy child's play or doing crafts. For the rest of us, simply loving our children and helping them be their best selves is enough.

In the meantime, I'm rebuilding my mom community and making plans with as many stay-at-home parents I can find. This parenting journey is much more enjoyable when shared with friends. I still clean and bake, and with my spare time I occasionally browse the parenting blogs and Facebook. I've learned, however, to limit my time. And I'm no longer so fearful of Pinterest. I might feel like a bad cook with an ugly house, but at least "bad mother" is off the list.

# 11. How Did a Golden Retriever End Up With Three Chocolate Labs?

*By Dawn*

Before having children, we had dogs – Casey, a docile golden retriever, and Hershey, an extremely energetic chocolate lab. Casey was a cream puff. He did what he was told and never caused us any trouble. Hershey, on the other hand, had a mind of her own. Trying to control her behavior, we took her to puppy kindergarten, which she failed – twice. We then hired a trainer to come to the house. He was so bewildered by her behavior that even he was left with only one suggestion: the zap collar. So we reluctantly outfitted her with a collar that we'd zap every time she acted up. Even that didn't work. The damn dog did exactly as she pleased.

Though I loved both dogs, I connected better with Casey. I could leave Casey at home with free range. Hershey, however, could not be unattended as she wreaked havoc on our house – chewing windowsills, devouring throw rugs like they were sirloin steaks and breaking anything within a paw's reach. The last straw for me came the day she destroyed my brand-new polarized sunglasses. I'd just gotten them with a voucher from work because I wanted to replace my Ray-Ban knockoffs. There they sat in a mangled pile, lenses chewed to pieces. I wanted to cry. My husband tried to blame me for leaving them in a careless place. Who knew the kitchen counter wasn't a safe space? I had no idea how to control this crazed animal, so I sat back and watched her live out her mission to devastate my home, one room at a time.

In deciding whether to have children, never, ever did it occur to me that not one, but all three of my brood would be like Hershey; way more than I could handle.

Casey and I are the rule followers. We do what we're supposed to do. Growing up I would have been known as a "compliant child." Once I found out I was pregnant, I did everything my doctor and society advised: gave up dangerous food and drink; took childbirth classes, prepared the nursery, etc. Once my son was born, I turned to the experts: Dr. Brazelton, Dr. Sears and TLC's "The Baby Channel." As instructed, I breastfed him, stimulated him with music and endless readings of *Good Night Moon*, gave him the requisite daily minutes of tummy time; placed him on his back to sleep and introduced solids at exactly six months. Everything was going well, so I logically assumed his development would proceed smoothly. And it did, for the first five years.

When the time came for kindergarten, my husband and I chose to enroll him in a Catholic school. As a working mom I needed a full-day program, and this school had a fantastic reputation with small class sizes and wonderful teachers. My child seemed fairly intelligent, so I wanted to take full advantage of his potential. Also, I smugly assumed that my child's learning might be thwarted by other children's behavioral problems. Ha! The joke was on me. My child ended up being the problem. He constantly interrupted the class with his fidgeting and endless questions. His report cards, which I always assumed would be filled with glowing comments about my brilliant child, instead were riddled with complaints – he couldn't stop fidgeting; he didn't raise his hands; he had difficulty taking turns. Notes came home … NOTES! *Mrs. M., please remind your son that he is not allowed to …* I began to get anxious each day as I emptied his backpack, waiting for another note that would riddle me with confusion – what do I do with a child who doesn't follow the rules? Worse, what if he got kicked out of school?

Finally, a family friend, who also happened to be a teacher, pulled me aside and gingerly suggested that perhaps my son had "a touch" of ADHD. I'd heard the term ADHD, but it wasn't as prevalent in 2005 as it is today. My only image of the disorder resembled that of a high-strung poodle that had just broken off its leash. That image did not give me solace, "touch" or not. And what exactly did "a touch" mean? Was it like "a touch" of diabetes where one has to watch his sugar but could eat the occasional chocolate cake? Did merely "a touch" of something mean it could be managed? Would my child have the potential for a healthy, successful life?

Following my friend's advice, we took my son to be evaluated. The evaluation site did not help ease my anxiety, as it was not in the safest of areas; fences surrounded the building with signs that read, "Secure All Valuables." Across the street I recognized a housing development from the news, as someone had been shot there during a gang fight. After locking the car three times, I gripped my son's small hand and entered the dismal building. Why did places dealing with such serious issues have to be so depressing?

While there we met with three different doctors and were given a barrage of forms to be filled out. My son meanwhile underwent a rigorous full day of testing, with a short break for lunch. Returning to the center four weeks later, we learned that indeed our son had ADHD. Overwhelmed, I burst into tears. Here it was: a label for my son; a label that meant my child would suffer from a problem that had the potential to negatively impact his entire life. Drugs, therapy and endless doctor visits awaited us. I felt like a failure, even though I knew deep down it had nothing to do with me. After all, I did everything in my power to give my child a healthy start in life, but could I have done more?

The doctors assured me that everything would be okay. They slid a box of Kleenex toward me, reminding me that other parents had probably experienced a reaction similar to mine. They reviewed the test results and how they arrived at their diagnosis. They then advised us to use a combination of therapy and medication, a regimen we would follow for the indefinite future.

I naturally felt leery about starting such a young child on medication. What would be the future effects on his mental and physical well-being? The doctors suggested that therapy alone would help, but my son would most likely be too frustrated to implement the strategies he'd learn. Medication would allow him to cope. Knowing I needed to provide him with the best defense available, I relented and opted for the drugs.

Never in my wildest dreams did I imagine that obtaining this medication would be more difficult than scoring methamphetamines outside a police station. They're controlled substances, meaning you can't just phone in the prescription or use the automated system to get a refill. At each and every visit to the pharmacy, I must present the actual written prescription. Then I wait. Often to pass the time I engage in mundane activities like taking my blood pressure repeatedly to see if waiting for a prescription causes it to increase. It's not all bad; I do get to scan the latest magazines. Should I get yet another subscription to add additional reading material to my collection at home?

Sometimes, while my arm is in the cuff, I'm told that the medications are not in stock. This means the statewide hunt begins, and the blood pressure goes up! I've traveled from one end of the state to the other, just to get my prescription filled. Once I get to the pharmacy, I must present an ID and my name goes in the pharmacist's "special book." Who else is in there? Michael Jackson? Lindsay Lohan? Getting my child his seemingly benign medication has always been a process.

The good news is that the medication began to work. My son paid attention in class without being disruptive. The report cards glowed. Then, a few years later, my second child received the same diagnosis. My daughter's diagnosis came as a complete shock and surprise because she had always been an easy baby, able to soothe herself, with a calm and laid-back demeanor, content to sit and take it all in. My son, on the other hand, the King of Colic, had also been a wild toddler who got into everything. I can't deny, however, that once my daughter entered school, she too began to have similar focusing issues. Unlike her brother, who was always in his head, she was hypersensitive to her environment. Like *The Mentalist*, she could reiterate every detail of a room and its inhabitants if asked, while my son would ask "What room?" Nonetheless, the diagnosis and treatment were the same.

My last child exhibited no obvious symptoms, just little signs here and there; enough so that we knew an evaluation was in our future. Sure enough – ADHD times three. Unlike the other two, however, we did not put her on medication because her case, being mild, did not seriously affect her performance in school. This meant I would have to deal with endless cartwheels in the kitchen and incessant chatter, but at least it's one less child on meds.

How am I coping? If you saw me on the street and asked, "How's it going?" my response would be rote: "Great." Inside, however, I am floundering in a sea of bedlam. I'm in the movie *Groundhog Day*, where each morning I awake to the same, unforgiving challenges.

My alarm wakes me up at 6:30 a.m. After having my first cup of coffee, I get the kids out of bed and urge them downstairs. From the moment they set foot out of their bedrooms, the fighting begins – who gets in the bathroom first; who eats the last bit of Honey Nut Cheerios; who chooses the show they watch on Nickelodeon. I've tried changing my routine, which includes getting them up at different times, having lots of their favorite cereals on hand and keeping the TV off. Sadly, the result is the same – they just find something different to fight about. Each morning when I hear that alarm, I anticipate that my kids' behavior will be tolerable, and yet it never is. I keep wondering if there's a life lesson I should be learning and maybe, if I get it right one of these days; like Bill Murray's character in the movie, I'll be free. It never happens. I've thought about calling the Super Nanny, but parenting live on camera while someone shouts "Action!" is more than I can bear.

I have found some comfort in learning that kids with ADHD tend to be more intelligent, more creative. I agree and am happy my kids possess these important attributes. Even still, my husband and I have joked, "A little dumb wouldn't hurt." I've also been told that their strong-willed nature will serve them well later in life, especially if they decide to pursue a career in politics or the law. Wonderful. So as adults they'll either be highly argumentative or prone to scandal.

At one point we had contemplated joining a group called CHADD – a support group for parents of kids with ADHD –but it fell on my husband's card night, so the option of saying, "My name is Dawn and my kids have ADHD" was not for me. Truth be told, however, it would have been nice to know I wasn't the only one out there. No one talks openly about these issues. This is not the type of things moms mention at birthday parties and play dates. Having "less than perfect" kids is a private matter. The ADHD, the therapy, the meds – all of it stays in the closet, feeling eerily like a dark, shameful secret.

Also, part of me has felt that my kids' problems are personal to them; I therefore have no right to share them. Their issues come under the rubric of mental health, to which there is definitely a stigma attached. Keeping this secret for so long, however, has taken its toll on me. I'm left feeling so lonely and isolated. However, once I opened up to other women, some of them strangers, I found out the honest truth – I am not alone. Not even close. As my newfound friends and I shared out stories, we laughed at our similarities and our children's misfortunes. Laughter feels so much better than emptiness.

My friend Carol recently shared her personal story with me. She has three children, one of whom has selective mutism, the other – oppositional defiant disorder (ODD). The fate of her youngest remains at bay.

Her son with ODD directs all his rage toward his mother, swearing at her and calling her fat. Her daughter, on the other hand, expresses her anger differently, by remaining silent. She has selective mutism, meaning she doesn't speak, even though she's physically capable of doing so. I personally had no idea her daughter suffered from such an affliction. I, like most in Carol's social circle, assumed the girl was simply shy or withdrawn. We probably all thought her son was just extremely disrespectful. Instead their personalities have a diagnosis – one that places a label on a troubled child and pressure on the parents to make everything better.

When I first heard the term "selective mutism," I thought, "How wonderful – a child who doesn't talk," especially since mine never stop talking. That wonderment quickly wore off when I learned more. Although her daughter is quiet and withdrawn in social situations, at home she is quite the opposite: bossy, domineering and moody. For example, she refuses to wear anything but jeans and sneakers, so any event they attend, no matter how fancy or special, her daughter is under-dressed. Carol ends up on the receiving end of a look that says "I can't believe she let her daughter wear that to this event!" As the mother, she's deemed the failure.

It's ironic – we scrutinize ourselves ruthlessly while thinking other people's children are so perfect. Yet once parents speak frankly, you realize kids are all the same. If it's not colic, ADHD or ODD, it's a food allergy or a medical condition. How many kids do you know who have undergone some type of physical, occupational or speech therapy, or even the cocktail of all three? My middle child had physical therapy because she didn't crawl on schedule. One friend's son was sent to physical therapy because he was not terribly coordinated at the tender age of four. My friend's response: "Of course he's not coordinated; have you seen me dance?"

Knowing most of our kids suffer from one problem or another, it would be great if we could all relax, show some empathy and cut our fellow sisters some slack. Instead of judging that woman in Target who's screaming at her unruly child, wouldn't it be better to give her a smile that says, "We've all been there"? Rather than feel superior to the parent whose kid forgot to turn in his homework, could we send a vibe of sympathy toward them both?

One day last summer, I was dropping off my kids at camp. I pulled up to the curb and opened the door to get the kids out as quickly as possible, since the drop-off line was beginning to form behind me. Rather than jump out of the car and run eagerly toward camp, my children sat in the car, slapping each other, screaming about who got the last lemonade and who was stuck with the apple juice box. They caused such a ruckus that the other families turned to stare. As I tried to yank them out of the car, a woman I've never met walked by and said, "Can't you give your mom a break?" I wanted to run up and kiss her. I felt validated, and in that instant did not feel like a deadbeat parent who couldn't control her kids.

Knowing what I know, I too pay homage to all the unspoken truths. I now make a point to offer that knowing smile to every struggling parent I encounter. I'm more open about my issues and feelings. I offer a heartfelt prayer to each and every parent, even the perfect ones. Perhaps with continued honesty, the company of wonderful friends and the support of a community, someday I might even shout, "Isn't motherhood great?" and mean it.

# III. THE RING TEST FAILED ME.

*By Kim*

"I really didn't care," said the excessively large pregnant woman to her friend as she pushed her young son on the swing. "I mean it, I didn't care. Everyone kept saying to me, 'You must have a preference,' but I really didn't care. Whatever God gives me, I'm happy. I really didn't care."

I'm not sure who she was trying to convince, but she certainly didn't convince me. Anyone who says "I really didn't care" that many times in one minute cares a whole heck of a lot. I assumed she was talking about the gender of her baby – another boy – and trying to convince herself that she didn't mind being stuck again in the land of blue. But I assumed wrong because in her next sentence, she revealed that she was having a daughter and she'd already ordered the **Disney Princess crib**.

This woman's willingness, nay desire, to place her new baby in a Disney Princess crib is proof positive that she gave a *huge* shit about the sex of her unborn baby. She is clearly setting that child up for a lifetime of pink tulle and headbands and praying for, not just a girl, but a girlie-girl. If that's the case, why did she desperately need to convince her friend, and herself, that she didn't care about her child's gender? Why is it so wrong to admit that you'd prefer to raise a child of one gender over the other?

When I bring up this topic with other moms, I'm surprised at how quickly and candidly they admit their feelings, yet it seems they're admitting them publicly for the first time. The topic feels taboo because you're only supposed to want a healthy baby, right?

A friend of mine recently admitted to me that she burst into tears at her ultrasound when she found out her baby was a girl. These were not, mind you, tears of joy. At the time she was the mom to two challenging teenage girls, and adding more estrogen to her home seemed unthinkable. She told me that once her daughter was born, all feelings of longing for a boy disappeared. We often wonder if her daughter sensed something because at age six she is a certifiable tomboy who loves Thomas the Train and dinosaurs. She has even expressed a desire to accompany her daddy on his next hunting trip, asking him, "What kind of cow do we have to kill to get ham?" I love that she's willing to kill any animal – pig or cow – just to get herself some nitrate-filled meat.

I never had a gender preference, though truthfully, I've always thought of myself as a boy mom. I just love little boys – their rough-and-tumble nature, lack of drama, and ease with which they go about the world. So I was not surprised when I bore my first child and it had a penis. I loved my little boy and did not give one thought to what I was missing on the little girl scene.

Two years later, I was pregnant with my second child and, given my age and several miscarriages, I could only think of having a healthy baby. Once I passed the first trimester and everything looked fine, however, I started thinking about the baby's gender. I loved the surprise with my first child, and again chose to let my second child's gender remain a secret. Everyone I encountered guessed that I was having a girl (i.e., your ass is getting really fat) and very gender test online I took said the same. A friend with a ninety percent success rate at guessing gender did her ring test on me. She hung my wedding ring from a string over my belly. It began moving in circles as opposed to side to side. Circular motions mean you're having a girl. I guess I was having a girl.

Had my first child been a girl I would have been scared to death. I am a highly competitive person with some serious father issues, so I feared my reaction if my daughter preferred her daddy over me, or worse, he preferred her. And my relationship with my mom, although close, is sometimes fraught with drama and emotion. My brother, on the other hand, seems to enjoy an easy, loving relationship with her.

Boys always love their moms. They may flee the nest and not come back, but they will never hold a grudge. They forgive easily and laugh off mom's craziness. Not daughters. We hold onto every little thing Mom says to us. We take it personally and want apologies. We look contemptuously at our mother's shortcomings and say "That won't be me!" Daughters are tough on their moms.

The prospect of having a daughter terrified me, but, because everyone guessed I was having a girl, I began to get used to the idea. I even became excited about her arrival and began to picture the mini-me that would soon arrive. Would she be doomed with my short torso and complete lack of waist? Would she inherit my husband's full lips? Would she sit peacefully for hours at a time, drawing pictures of rainbows and unicorns? Would she be a sweet, agreeable child who hated princesses but adored her brother? Now this child had some promise.

My husband and I picked out a name that was both strong and feminine, exactly as she would be. She would wear striped tights and pink Chuck Taylors. Snow White would be her favorite Disney character because she's the coolest – hanging with the Seven Dwarves and being brunette and all. I felt some sadness for the younger brother my son would never know, but hoped his little sister would bring home some hot friends and he'd forgive me. I started to adore her. I started to have dreams that her young life would be all that mine wasn't. She would avoid my pitfalls and mistakes based on all the sage advice I'd provide her. She would grow to be a strong, confident woman.

During my second pregnancy, people said things to me they never did during my first pregnancy, like, "I hope you have a girl. Every woman needs a daughter," or "Perfect family – one of each." They would provide me with little quips like "Daughter for life, lose a son to his wife," or promise to hand down great quality girl clothes. Let me remind you that I never had an ultrasound showing I was having a girl; these were comments I received courtesy only of my big fat ass. I heard these things so often that I truly believed I was having a girl. We didn't even choose a boy's name.

Given my age, the doctors insisted I go for non-stress tests, so at thirty-seven weeks I arrived for my ultrasound, annoyed at the inconvenience but excited to get a glimpse of my baby. As the ultrasound tech ran the cool wand over my belly I flinched and said, "Oh, I almost forgot to tell you. I don't know the sex of the baby and don't want to know." She laughed and said, "Well then you'd better not look now."

Nine months of curiosity and I couldn't wait one more second. Besides, I thought, could the untrained eye really decipher genitals on an ultrasound? I recall being told I was looking at feet, eyes, and hands and it all looked like a freaky alien to me. So I looked, thinking I'd leave as clueless as I came.

There they were in all their glory: the family jewels. There was no mistaking what I was seeing. I was, after all, a woman of forty-two who'd been around the block a few times and therefore seen balls and penises from many different angles. It was such an arrogant display, as though he had pressed his junk against the camera saying, "So you think you're having a daughter? Guess again, Mama!"

I stared at the screen and asked, "Is that what I think it is?" "Yes!" she exhorted. "You're having a boy!" I thought to myself that I must be seeing someone else's ultrasound. The ring test told me I was having a girl. I felt betrayed.

I called my husband as soon as I left and he asked me how I felt about it. "I'm fine," I told him. "Why would I be otherwise?" On the way home I stopped to pick up a birthday card for my mom. As I perused the aisle of mother-daughter cards I broke down sobbing and had to leave the store. My behavior humiliated me so I dried my eyes before facing my husband. He hugged me hard and asked me again how I was doing. "Fine," I replied again with an agitated tone.

"I know we thought it was a girl so I just want to make sure you're not disappointed."

"The baby is healthy! Do you know how lucky we are?" I screamed at him and then bawled all over again, tears staining his shoulders. I cried for my disappointment, for the shame I felt in wanting a daughter, for the sadness my unborn little boy would experience if he knew the ugly truth about his mother.

I spent the next week in a fog. Anytime someone asked if I was having a boy or a girl, I pasted a sadistic smile on my face and gave them my rote response: "Don't know! We love a surprise!" I continued to get "Looks like a girl to me" comments, which I choked on with a smirk.

At my next midwife appointment, I told her what happened. It felt like a safe thing to do in her earthy-crunchy home with her patent acceptance of all things hormonal. She listened sympathetically, gave me a hug and told me that my feelings were normal.

My daughter became real in my dreams and now she was gone, and I needed to grieve the loss.

My midwife's acceptance of my ugliness helped immensely, though I have to admit that "grieving" for a child that never existed felt somewhat self-indulgent. Shouldn't grieving be reserved for women who'd lost actual babies? Like all feelings, however, mine needed to be processed, no matter how self-absorbed this felt. So I did just that as I began to accept the fact that my last child would be a boy.

We picked a name, as equally cool as our girl name and a fantastic match to his brother's, at least according to BabyCenter.com. I rejoiced at the money I'd save by recycling clothes and toys, and thought of all the ways I'd spend that money on myself. I appreciated the scores of girlfriends I had, both old and new, as well as a sister, sisters-in-law and cousins, all of whom fulfill my need for female companionship - completely. Who needs a daughter when you have so many wonderful chicks in your life?

I wish I could say that was the end of the story, but alas, no. To my shock and horror, the issue resurfaced the day my son was born, albeit momentarily. His birth was perfect, taking place at home, as planned, in the mid-morning hours after a short but intense labor. I felt his head descend down the birth canal and my husband grabbed his little hand, which was holding his own cheek, while he was still inside of me. He entered this world through the warm water of a birth tub and his slippery brand new body was placed in my waiting arms. There was no surprise when I saw his penis. I felt resolved. I also felt a millisecond of disappointment as I'd hoped that the ultrasound was wrong. Luckily it dissipated when he nursed for the first time. I drank in his beauty and his unique nature and fell in love. But make no mistake, my friends, I felt the disappointment, and still do from time to time. These feelings have nothing to do with my son. They are all about my non-existent daughter.

Why didn't anyone tell me I might feel this way? Why doesn't anyone admit these feelings? Other parents I've spoken to will, if probed, admit they wanted a child of a specific gender. Every one of those people, however, tells me that once the child is born, those feelings of disappointment or desire go away. I don't believe them. Why the façade?

As difficult as it is for me to admit publicly, I'm hopelessly and irrevocably saddened by the fact that I will never have a daughter. I strangely never felt this way until my second pregnancy, when everyone felt the need to share their words of wisdom and quips about mother/daughter relationships. I know I shouldn't care what others say, but their words hit a nerve. Though I'm grateful for what I have - two healthy, smart, beautiful boys – I am also an American. We're taught that we can have it all if we just try hard enough, if we just believe and stay positive. That's the American Dream. But when we don't give birth to our preferred gender, we are expected to be grateful that our kids are healthy and ask for no more, which sounds vaguely un-American.

This conundrum is further complicated by society's interest in our personal lives. We are asked when we will get married the minute we start a serious relationship. Once married, the inquiry continues with questions of offspring. Once a baby arrives, the question changes to one of curiosity about adding to the brood. Next come the hopes of others that you will have a boy if you already have a girl, and vice-versa. If you are married and have two children, one boy and one girl, you have achieved a fictitious state of perfection in which people will blissfully leave you alone because they are satisfied with your life's achievements.

Believe it or not, I'm forty-four and people still ask me if I'm going to try for a girl. Or I hear things like, "Maybe you'll have a wonderful daughter-in-law," or "Perhaps one of your sons will be gay," as if these potential outcomes are my consolation prize. One family member who lavished over me during my second pregnancy and promised me the beautiful girl hand-me-downs has never acknowledged the birth of my second son. Would the result have been different if he'd been a girl?

All of this is insulting on many levels, but mostly because it sends a message that my life is not complete because I don't have a daughter. In some sense this is true. I will miss out on all the wonderful experiences I've had with my own mother. Yes, we've had our drama, but we've also shared so much and been extremely close and those are the memories that I hold dearest.

My boys will live their lives and I will become an afterthought. They will always love me, but they will not want to share the intimate details of their lives with me. They will not get excited about shopping trips, high tea or a weekend in New York with their mom. Those pleasantries are reserved for mothers and daughters. It's a club to which I will never belong, which is so odd to me because I've actually been in the club my whole life. Do I get kicked out when my mother dies? Also, no matter how wonderful my future daughter-in-law might be, let's be real. I will never be the most favored grandmother to her grandchildren, sanctimoniously stealing them from the annoying in-laws during the holidays. Instead, I am the annoying in-law.

When I look at my two-year-old second son, I can't imagine having a different child. He's quite charming and can send me into fits of love that make me feel like my heart will explode. He loves to snuggle and is never stingy with his hugs and kisses. When I say "my boys," it feels right; this is the family I'm meant to have.

Who knows what might have been. With children, there are no guarantees. Their future is theirs alone and we can only hope to give them the tools they need to live the best life they can. We cannot demand that they take care of us or be our spa buddies. We should not lay a guilt trip if they choose to eat Christmas dinner with their in-laws because they happen to be more fun or better cooks.

At some point, most of us will grieve for the loss of some dream we had for our children. Our daughters could decide to be professional surfers when we dreamed of them being doctors. Our boys could end up loving other boys and choose not to have offspring possessing their sense of humor and sea-blue eyes. They might turn out to be people we plain old don't like and we, as their parents, have only one choice: acceptance.

At a midwife appointment, pre-birth but post-peep-show, she handed me a copy of the movie *It's a Wonderful Life*. She told me that she watched the movie and instantly thought of me because George Bailey is one of two boys, both of whom loved their mom and held her aloft on their shoulders in celebration of their family. She said this with tears in her eyes and I joined her, accepting my journey as the future mom to be left behind, but loved unconditionally.

It's a wonderful life indeed.

# IV. YOU CALL THIS A VACATION???

*By Dawn*

"How was your vacation?" my friend Lynne asked. A group of us from high school had gotten together for dinner and we were catching up on the events of the past winter.

Chrissi, a tall, bubbly schoolteacher, who seemed to adore spending time with her children, began gushing about her recent family ski trip in Maine. I, on the other hand, sat mute. We too had gone skiing for school break, but my experience was not something I wanted to share with my friends. Nothing awful happened. There was no major drama, but our week away with the kids felt more like a burden than a vacation. Was there something wrong with me? Chrissi has two kids; I have three – does that one extra child really make the difference? Maybe it's because she's a natural who loves kids, and me, well, not so much. The idea of running a daycare or teaching pre-school has never entered my mind.

As I listened to Chrissi talk about the how much she enjoyed her vacation, a hard truth presented itself: she loved her vacation, not because of the time she spent with her children, but rather the time she had to herself. During the day her kids skied with their friends and at night they played video games and pool at the bar, while the parents chatted and drank beer. My vacation didn't go so smoothly. The biggest difference between Chrissi's successful vacation and my failure was her ability to get rid of her children most of the time. Chrissi and I had the same vacation goals. I simply failed in achieving mine, as you'll plainly see…

School break was fast approaching and my husband and I wanted to take the kids away for a few days. Rather than take out a second mortgage on our home and go to Disney, we decided to stay local and go skiing. My kids had enjoyed their previous skiing experience, and I loved it because it reminded me of those carefree years: my twenties. We would pile a group of our closest friends into a house with one bathroom, and I always skied with my fellow novice ski buddy and co-author. We laughed when our butts stuck to the chair lift as we dismounted and didn't care that we looked like old ladies plodding down the mountain at a snail's pace. Neither of us skied as kids, putting us at a serious disadvantage to our fellow housemates, but none of that mattered. The fresh air felt wonderful after so many winter days spent indoors. I went home feeling refreshed and invigorated, ready to face another week.

I wanted my kids to experience that same rush of energy I did from skiing. I wanted them to be good skiers as adults so they would never feel left out. Most importantly, I wanted to create wonderful memories for my children of long days on the slopes and fun family time at night. So we booked a ski rental with two other couples and their kids, thinking this would make it even more fun.

Our condo was in a resort town in New Hampshire, which had plenty of restaurants, shopping and activities to keep the kids busy. I signed the kids up for ski school, mostly because I am not skilled enough to teach them to ski. Also, I needed some down time – from work *and* from my family. I run a fairly busy optometry practice where I'm on my feet most of the day. Truthfully I'm bored out of my mind repeating the same mantra day in and day out: "Better one or better two?" It's so dull that I feel a rush of excitement when I find a potential tumor or some herpes of the eye.

My worst day at work, however, is less depleting than a day with my kids. Aside from their constant demands, they fight like animals in the wild. My oldest loves to goad his sisters. The girls fight about absolutely everything. Each day I hear the familiar taunts: He took my iPod! She hit me! She changed the channel on the radio! She's wearing my sweater! She's using my hairbrush! It never ends.

I needed a vacation and foolishly thought this trip might provide me with the respite I so desperately needed. I especially looked forward to our first day with the kids in all-day ski school. Imagine – six and a half hours of freedom to ski, read a book by the fire, have a cocktail – the possibilities were endless.

We got to the mountain and made our way over to the ski school corral. I put the girls in level two classes and my son in level three with his buddies. My friends and I kissed our kids goodbye and skied away. I felt the familiar sensation of exhilaration I always felt when I finally get some time to myself – one you can only feel when you've also experienced deprivation. As a working mom, my time away from my kids is mostly when I'm at work, so when I get some actual time to myself, it's positively delicious – like the first glass of wine after nine long months of pregnancy, an unexpected warm day in the middle of winter or eating that chocolate Easter bunny after giving up candy for Lent. Yeah, it's that good.

I hit the mountain and slowly re-acclimated to the swaying and balancing that comes with skiing while the sun shone on my face. I was so happy I didn't care that my rosacea would become inflamed. A couple of hours into my skiing, a familiar sound came from my jacket pocket. Was that my cell phone? Who would bother me on my day off? I pulled out the phone and saw an unfamiliar area code.

I answered it, foolishly, to be met with the devastating news that my middle child wanted to quit her ski lesson. Her instructor informed me that she hated skiing and was ready to quit. Panic and frustration set in as I saw my future unfolding before me ... a day in the lodge with my ten-year-old complaining about her boredom. I pleaded with the instructor to force her to ski. She promised to keep trying for at least another half hour, but in the meantime, we agreed to meet at the corral.

While I made my way, enthusiasm deflating, I mulled over the true impact of retrieving my daughter from ski school early. If she quit, that would probably mean the other two wouldn't want to ski either. What would we do all afternoon? What about later in the week? My mind started racing. This was my vacation too, wasn't it? Don't they deal with other kids who don't love skiing at first? But I couldn't stop running the instructor's words through my head: "She hates it." I know how she gets when she's made up her mind.

Once I made it back to the corral, I anxiously scoped the field and didn't see my daughter, so I checked in and was told that she turned a corner and all was well. I exhaled, knowing the day was mine again. As I skied toward the gondola a mere two minutes later, the familiar sound emanated from my pocket yet again – the dreaded cell phone.

This time it was my son's instructor. He informed me that my previously healthy son now had a stomachache and wanted to go inside and rest.

Really, now. My son never gets stomachaches. I can smell a faker from miles away, but how do I explain this to the instructor?

Had I truly believed he was sick, I would have been much more sympathetic. Ditto if I truly believed that my daughter was miserable. But I know my kids and I wasn't fully convinced one child was experiencing flu-like symptoms, nor that the other hated skiing. What I am convinced of is that they are classic manipulators, willing to use any weapon in their arsenal to get their way. Their tricks don't work on me, but these ski instructors were fresh meat. How could I make them see that my kids' complaining was all a ruse to get out of the cold and into the lodge? Suck it up and make them ski!

I conveyed this to the instructor as best I could without sounding like a cold-hearted bitch. To my relief, I learned my son was willing to overlook his stomach bug and ski again. The day finished uneventfully and the kids told me they enjoyed the skiing. What they didn't enjoy, however, was seeing their friends ski off without them. After their skills were assessed, my son was demoted to level two with his sisters, making all three of them miserable. I knew it! There was no stomach bug. There was no hatred of the sport. It was my kids reacting when they didn't get their way. I was relieved to know that my kids would ski again, though they all begged for a private lesson. My husband and I could have flown to Colorado for the weekend for the cost of that private lesson, but I was willing to do anything to get them away from me.

On the morning of their lesson we met their instructor, Skip. I warned him that he'd have to be tough with them. My children responded to structure and if they're pampered, they claim the upper hand. He nodded, acting like he understood exactly what I was saying, and off they went. He looked weak. I smelled disaster.

Being an optimist, I booked a ski lesson for myself along with my ski-house friends. An hour into my lesson and there was that freaking cell phone with the unfamiliar area code. It was Skip. My youngest refused to go on the chair lift and he wanted me to meet them at the base of the kiddie slope.

What about *my* ski lesson? I had just begun to master leaning forward with the imaginary grape on the back of my leg. The next hour would be about planting a pole in the imaginary box that encircled me. These were skills that were essential to the mastering of the blue trails. I wanted to ski a blue trail! My fellow skiers, after witnessing the barrage of never-ending phone calls and complaining from my pain-in-the-ass kids, smiled at me and turned toward the gondola, their cell phones silent and their children entertained. They must have been getting tired of all the drama.

I tried to act mature, but truthfully I felt cheated. I went with my daughter on the chair lift and found she only needed me to join her one time to build her confidence on the lift. At the bottom of the mountain she said, "I'm OK, Mom. You can go back to your lesson." Thanks kid, but my lesson is on the other side of the world, and over.

After a harried lunch, clomping around in ski boots and trying to carry two trays of over-priced grilled cheese and fries, I dumped the kids with Skip to finish their lesson and rejoined my friends to attempt a final shot at skiing with the adults. Just as we hit the gondola line, I kid you not, my friends, that motherfucking phone started to ring. This time, my middle child had a meltdown and sat on the mountain refusing to ski. "Leave her!" I ranted. "She just wants attention." Skip refused, clearly having fallen victim to my daughter's spell. Fortunately another instructor took pity on the situation and dragged her skiing. No balls on that Skip, just like I suspected.

I called my husband, who'd stayed back at the condo, to ask him to take over cell phone duty. He didn't seem pleased that

I was disturbing his vacation. After all, he needed to relax. But he showed up, begrudgingly, and took my cell phone so I could have a couple of hours to myself, ring-free.

The rest of the vacation went similarly. One day we rented snow tubes. Sounds simple enough, right? Nothing, however, is simple with my kids. My youngest daughter wanted to go down the mountain with me, but they only allowed single riders. Back and forth we went; she complained, I explained the rules. She didn't like the rules and continued to complain. Finally, after thirty-five minutes and much negotiation, she relented, went down by herself, and loved it. What kid wouldn't? I don't know why everything has to be so much work.

Even the pool didn't provide a respite, despite the fact that all three of my kids love to swim. I watched my friends sit poolside, reading or chatting while their kids swam. I, on the other hand, had to respond to the incessant calls of "Mommy, watch this!" with each lame jump into the pool. Sorry kid, but you're no Michael Phelps.

On our last day of vacation, I couldn't get our bags in the car fast enough. Going home to a stack of laundry and a pile of bills felt so much more appealing than one more day on that damn mountain.

Later that night I took a few minutes to reflect – are vacations worth it? In reality, yes. My children will have fabulous memories of going away with their family and friends. They will have mastered a skill that will serve them well through the years. They won't remember the chaos and mishaps along the way. Life's about memories and we remember things the way we want to – pain-free and joyful.

I'm learning to lower my expectations. Have you ever seen those Royal Caribbean ads – the ones where the families are sitting together at dinner, laughing and having a grand old time? Ads like that set us up for the false belief that, if we go on a cruise, or to a resort, everyone will mysteriously get along and life will be blissfully simple and fun. It's crap. As a matter of fact, I'm not quite sure you can call that three- to fourteen-day break from everyday life "vacation," as it bears absolutely no resemblance to my pre-children escape from reality. It should be called "relocation" instead, because all our family problems and obligations just follow me to a different and unfamiliar place. The Go-Gos would never sing a song about this experience.

Is this a problem? Is there something wrong with us as parents that we need to ditch our kids just to relax and have some fun? Or is modern parenting so ridiculously demanding that a respite is essential to the survival of the human race?

As a child of the '70s, I remember a much different reality for my parents, as they had a full life that did not always include me. Every Saturday night they went out, leaving me with a sitter who had never been certified in CPR or taken a course in babysitting. They went on vacation without me and, if they took me along on their vacations, you can bet the trip did not revolve around entertaining Yours Truly. We never had a family meeting, asking where I'd like to go and what activities I'd like to do while away. I went where they took me, and did what they presented.

Life as a parent is quite different now and the result is that our children consume us. Everything we do is kid-friendly and controlled. So when we finally go on that once-a-year vacation, we want to let our hair down and feel free. We want, and need, a few hours in the day in which we can say, "I exist. I'm important." We want to feel like grown-ups again, and we deserve to do so, at least once a year.

As for this past "vacation," I've finally come to terms with its reality. I will smile politely when asked, "How was your vacation?" "Great!" I'll exclaim, hoping someday my vacation realities will morph into the vacation fantasies that got me into this mess in the first place.

# V. Rocket Science is for Wimps.

*By Kim*

"Poopie … butthole … diarrhea … penis." These are the latest additions to my two-year-old's limited vocabulary and he shares them with everyone he meets. It began last fall at a doctor's visit. Our usual doctor has three small children of her own, so she gets it. That day, unfortunately, we had the pleasure of the stoic doctor with the Russian accent, who was not at all amused by my children or my nervous banter. Naturally you can imagine her reaction when my two-year-old looked her in the face and said, "Butthole."

I gave the doctor a half smile, expecting her to acknowledge this developmental milestone, or perhaps praise my young son for his ability to enunciate such a difficult word at such a young age. The kid still said "wa-wa" for water and "cow" for car, but "butthole" came out loud and clear. He even accentuated the double "t" so there's no mistaking he's talking about an anus.

I received nothing of the sort, but instead met with a facial expression that said she was not amused. I once learned it's best to ignore the potty talk, so that's what I'm trying to do. I even explained this to her and was greeted with a half smile in return; that is until he said it again, a mere thirty seconds later, and continued until we were deluged with buttholes. At this point my older son was roaring with laughter, while I tried to contain the damage by offering the baby a toy car. It was too late. I am a no-good rotten mom in the eyes of this woman – one more in that column. The world is keeping score, and I am losing.

The potty talk period lasted for about four months. It began with an innocent outcry of "poopie." Not too many people get upset at hearing a two-year-old say "poopie" so I didn't think this behavior warranted a Google search or an afternoon with the parenting books. Somewhere along the way, however, he learned the word "butthole" – I can only assume it was a gift from his older brother. Butthole is a lot different than poopie. It conjures up images of a big, hairy, stinky ass. It has no business coming from the mouth of a two-year-old, even if my attempts to hide my smile say otherwise. My father-in-law made his displeasure very clear.

"Did your son just call me a butthole?" he asked my husband with his slight southern drawl (he's from Florida so I often think he's faking it, but regardless, hearing the word "butthole" said in a southern accent does not help make a funny situation more serious).

"No, Dad," he responded. "He's not *calling* you a butthole. He's just saying the word. It's what two-year-olds do." Apparently my father-in-law was unfamiliar with the normal development of a two-year-old because he promptly informed us that he didn't want to hear such talk in his house. I guess it was time to put an end to butthole (excuse the pun).

Have you ever tried to make a two-year-old do anything? It's a lot harder than it looks. "Redirect their behavior" is what I've been told, so I tried getting him to say "donut face" and "coffee head" instead. I would laugh with false bravado every time he uttered those words, and it worked, for a bit, until he heard the word "diarrhea." He had a case of the runs one day and I made the grave error of telling him he had diarrhea. It's a word that complements his others so well that he decided to start a mantra … "poopie … butthole … diarrhea." "Coffee head" no longer sounded so funny.

My brother found the retinue hilarious and is the one who suggested he add the word "penis." My neighbor heard the full mantra and laughed along with him, exclaiming "how adorable!" Family and friends did not help the situation, though truth be told, I too found it funny. I admired the way my pint-sized Andrew Dice Clay said these words with such audacity. At heart I'm a thirteen-year-old boy. I always laugh at a good fart. I have taught my kids to pull my finger and to blame their farts on one another; I have even Dutch-ovened them on more than one occasion. I can't help it.

Immaturity aside, however, I know this behavior should be contained to the home. My kids, on the other hand, want to share their humor with the world. The world is not so forgiving, as I have learned the hard way. The worst incident occurred on Election Day.

I always vote, even though I realize my vote doesn't count in the tiny blue state of Rhode Island. In 2012, nothing would have kept me from those polls – not even my two-year-old's reign of terror. That is why I refused to leave, despite the fact that my young son continued to repeat his mantra to every person in line at the polling place: poopie … butthole … diarrhea … penis.

The horror began with the woman behind me in line, the perfectly coiffed mom of two equally coiffed daughters. She gave me the scornful eye; the one that says I'm an embarrassment to womankind and should have my uterus yanked out immediately. Screw you, girl-mom. What do you know about poopies and buttholes? Your whole world right now is princesses and sparkly Uggs. I'm drowning in a sea of penises. The least you could do is throw me a smile. I hope one of your daughters gets pregnant in high school and ends up on that show about the teenage moms.

Not one person was amused. No one was supportive or understanding. I personified the mom who could not control her children. I knew deep down they're right, but what could I have done? Scream at him? Hit him? Put him on a leash and give him a muzzle? Other than leaving, my options were quite limited and I wanted to vote, damn it! So I tried in vain to redirect his behavior. (Can you talk about donuts instead? Aren't donuts funny, you donut face?) He could smell my desperation and the donuts had no chance. I left there humiliated. I felt frustrated by my inability to effectively parent my children, and confused about society's reaction to their developmentally normal behavior. Why is this so hard?

I'm not a dumb woman. I graduated high school with honors, despite the fact that I never studied. I endured law school and became an attorney. I read voraciously and do logic puzzles and Sudoku, for fun. I've always been fairly good at most things I've tried; a Jill of all trades, master of none. I guess I therefore assumed I'd know how to be a good parent. It's the only natural thing we do, right?

Wrong. Raising kids is ridiculously hard. How does the universe let this happen? No one would be allowed to perform brain surgery without the right skills, expertise and training. Never would one be sent to the O.R. with a scalpel and a few handbooks and told "good luck." Yet parenting, which feels like the mental equivalent of brain surgery, rocket science and the like, is treated like it's no big deal. Everything is a big deal, and each day I feel more clueless than the previous one.

Much of my time in public, I feel like I'm walking on eggshells: what will my kids do and how will the world react? As an adult, I have pretty much figured out how to behave in public: don't fart or burp – at least not intentionally – remain dressed at all times, don't be a close-talker, try not to verbally abuse strangers and always say "please" and "thank you." I don't do anything to make others raise an eyebrow or feel the need to reprimand me. In short, I am fully integrated into society from a behavioral point of view.

Now that I have children, however, I have no idea how to pass this integration onto them. People seem to be particularly vested in the behavior of my children and have a vast span of opinions regarding how they behave, which they are more than happy to share with me, not that I asked. I'm not talking about the farting and burping – that stuff usually gets a pass (pardon the pun, again). I'm talking about the everyday behavior – if they are too loud, too active, too fast, too jumpy, too snotty, too food-caked, too urine-smelling, too child-like. Everyone's watching me and I feel the pressure. Should I be militant mom who keeps her kids in line, or should I be freewheeling mom who lets her kids explore their world?

Either way I'm screwed. Often I'll be out in public thinking my kids are just being kids when I get "the look." You know it. It's often given by someone older who hasn't smiled in a decade. They either never had kids or had kids but never really liked them. The look says, "In my day, children were seen and not heard!" The look says that my children are obnoxious, and that terrifies me because I don't want to be the parent of the obnoxious children. After all, those parents always get blamed for their kids' behavior. So I rein them in accordingly.

In other situations I find myself trying to control what I perceive to be bad behavior when people smile at me and say,

"Don't worry – they're fine!" Then I feel like an uptight bitch who probably abuses her kids at home. I know they're thinking to themselves, "Give that woman a Xanax, please!" I can't win.

My husband Chris isn't much help because we have very different ideas on this one. He expects our kids to be quiet and respectful at all times. Before we were married, we had the misfortune of witnessing a freak of nature: four perfectly behaved children in a restaurant. I remember the scene with such clarity, as it really did seem unreal. The four kids were sitting quietly with their parents, enjoying the food and the conversation. Chris and I turned to the couple and asked, "What's your secret? Your kids are so well-behaved." They sort of shrugged their shoulders and said their kids always behaved this well.

Looking back, I wonder if perhaps those kids were lobotomized because I've yet to see children so quiet and accommodating in a restaurant, unless of course they have something electronic entertaining them. Or maybe those kids, like Lady Gaga, were born that way. The parents seemed to be sweet, wholesome people, probably from the Midwest or someplace where people are kind and polite to one another. Their children were most likely just following in their parents' footsteps.

If this was the secret, Chris and I had no hope. We are not laid back, sweet, trouble-free people. We were both born and raised in New England, meaning we naturally have that East Coast edge. To make matters worse, I come from a line of Italian women, all of whom are loud, emotional and opinionated. My husband, on the other hand, is of German descent, meaning his emotions are in check, but don't mess with him. We met in a bar in Boston, I as a newly divorced thirty-something lawyer and he as a twenty-nine-year-old who was "in between careers." He formerly worked as a bouncer at a popular Boston nightclub, where he'd been threatened at gunpoint, more than once. He was known to smoke cigarettes, drink Jack and Coke and wear faux leather pants. I was known to be buying bagels and coffee on a Sunday morning, still wearing the previous night's high heels. We are not the type of people who breed and create sweet, innocent, laid-back offspring, so I'm not quite sure why he's so surprised to find that our kids are not completely passive and restrained.

Whatever the reason, the bottom line is that he, in my opinion, has unreasonable expectations of our children, while I, in his opinion, do not discipline them harshly enough.

My fellow mothers don't offer much assistance on this issue either. I consider myself more of a free-range, laissez-faire kind of parent. I've never felt the need to follow my child around a playground, monitoring his every move. Other moms disagree with me, as evidenced by this all too familiar scenario:

"Whose child is this?" asks a fellow playground mom, pointing to my toddler who's happily playing on his own in the sand box.

"He's mine," I yell, looking up from my phone, a mere three feet away.

"Oh, well I was wondering 'cause he seemed to be alone."

"OK, thanks." I then feel like the bad, neglectful mom who is too busy playing solitaire on her iPhone to notice that her toddler is eating a shovel full of sand. Did I really need to be standing immediately at his side while he navigates the playground? Can't even our youngest citizens have a little bit of freedom to check out the world? I had one eye on him; just one, but one felt like enough.

It gets worse as the kids get older. In my opinion, children should gradually be given their independence. At a certain age, play dates and parties become drop-off affairs, though sadly not everyone feels the same way. A good friend once told me of bringing her son to a play date, expecting to drop him off and leave. The mom, however, insisted that she stay. They then proceeded to follow the children around from room to room while they played and the moms talked about, well, nothing interesting. What kind of message are we sending to those kids? They were six years old, by the way; far too old to choke on small toys or strangle themselves with electrical cords, but too young to break into the liquor cabinet. The only message such behavior sends is: We don't trust you. I want my kids to know that I trust them, unless and until they act like irresponsible assholes.

My older son is now six and quite frankly I don't have much more clarity on this issue. I'm content to leave him alone unless he's physically hurting someone, or being a bully. Truth be told, he is a tad bossy. Sometimes he treats his friends as his minions, engineering their play and telling them what they can and cannot do. His personality looks all too familiar, as I was definitely the ringleader of my three-chick childhood gang. The difference for me, however, was that adults were rarely around to monitor our play. I bossed my friends around and they followed me like little puppies. Every once in a while two of us ganged up on the third, but we all learned important lessons from those experiences, like negotiation and the rules of fair play.

Unfortunately for my son, however, I am almost always there, so I bear witness to his bossy behavior and physical play. I often hear other parents calling out his name. I'd been watching him and didn't notice anything that warranted parental interference, but clearly someone disagreed with me. Now I felt like I should go against my nature and be on hyper-alert; monitor my son's behavior and tell him he's being too rough, too mean, too bossy, too much himself. Sometimes I do, sometimes I don't, but I'm never quite sure what's right.

After one particularly stressful play session, I decided to sit down with my son and have a good, long talk about how we play with our friends. He listened in earnest but really didn't want to hear my thoughts on his play. Eventually he sighed and said, "You know what I wish? No grownups allowed!" I couldn't agree more, but that's not his reality in this day and age. Sorry bud, you should have been a kid in the '70s.

At the end of the day, I have no clue how much involvement is too much and how much is too little. When are my kids just being kids and when is their behavior inappropriate? No matter what path I choose, someone out there will disapprove of my parenting, for one reason or another.

I wish there were a handbook … OK, so there are a million handbooks and I've read a few here and there. The problem, however, is in the execution. Every parenting book I read, I nod along with the author, feeling a huge sense of relief that I finally have some guidance. I get excited and can hardly wait for my kids to wake up the next morning so I can practice my new skills. Typically within ten minutes, however, I'm unable to even remember what I read and I'm back to my old ways.

When I mention my confusion to friends, they always say, "Just do what you think is right." That's like telling a girl in middle school that it's OK to wear her pink "My Little Pony" sweatshirt because it's what she likes. While it's nice to be true to yourself, dealing with society's repercussions sucks the big one. No one wants to be the fourteen-year-old girl with a child's fashion sense. No one wants to be the mom with the undisciplined/over-disciplined child.

At the end of the day, I am the one responsible for my children's behavior. I feel confident that I can stop from them from eating their boogers, farting in public and being bullies. Other than that, it's a big guessing game for me. By the time I master this parenting thing, my kids will be grown and the blame will shift to them for their scandalous ways. Sadly I'll be old, and will probably start farting in public. Life really does go full circle.

# VI. MY HUSBAND'S GIRLFRIEND.

*By Dawn*

"I'm going to have to get myself a girlfriend," my husband chided as I rejected his nighttime advances, yet again. Sadly this has become a recurring theme in our household. Though to my knowledge, he's never made good on his threat, it does make me ponder: what role does sex play in a marriage once you have kids?

Let me begin by saying that I'm an extremely private person when it comes to my sex life. You would never see me reading *Fifty Shades of Grey* in public. I would never be the one making oral sex jokes at the sight of a banana or the mention of the number sixty-nine. I'm therefore going way out of my comfort zone to write this story, but I think it's one worth sharing. So here it goes …

Last summer I spent an afternoon at the beach with a group of friends, all of whom have children of varying ages. As the afternoon wore on and the wine buzz kicked in, the conversation got more lively and eventually turned to sex. There I sat mute once again, playing voyeur to other's intimacies. One of the moms, recently single, was in a new relationship and experiencing a revival of her sex life. The rest of us looked at her with a mix of envy and confusion. We envied her new excitement for getting down and dirty, but we were also confused: If sex sounds so great, why don't we want to do it more often? We all had partners who were more than willing, that's for sure. Most of us agreed that, no matter how much we liked sex, it was just the last thing on our minds at the end of the day. Our husbands, on the other hand, didn't seem to understand this reality. Instead they took our rejection of the sport as a personal affront, thereby ladling our already burdened consciences with more guilt.

One friend, Tiffany, offered some fantastic advice: "When I hear him coming into bed at night, I play 'dead possum.'" She then demonstrated her effective moves to the group, showing the lifeless face and limp arm-hang that looked disturbingly like, well, a dead possum.

We all pledged to try dead possum, even our dear friend Debbie, whose virulent husband expects sex every day. Yes, you read that right, every day. And if Debbie says, "No thanks," more than twice a week, she ends up on the receiving end of a lecture about how sex-starved he is, a lecture that typically took longer than the sex act itself, which is why she often acquiesced.

Poor Debbie was so over-sexed that she even looked forward to that time of the month. "Whenever I get my period I start doing a jig. I always lie and tell him it's longer than it is so he stays away. Is that pathetic?"

We all agreed no, her lie was not pathetic, and even tried to convince her to tell her husband she was becoming peri-menopausal, thereby getting her period every three weeks, or less.

"A little blood wouldn't deter my husband," said Tiffany. "Sometimes at night I hand him my arm and say 'Here, you can have an arm. That's it. The rest of me is going to sleep.'"

"Not much you can do with an arm," laughed Chrissi. "Or is there?" she mused. Tiffany did not respond, filling our heads with strange images.

This story is all too common among women. Let me rephrase that: This story is all too common among married women with children. There are many writings on the subject, ranging from one extreme to the other. In *365 Nights: A Memoir of Intimacy*[1], the author writes about having sex with her spouse every night for a year as a means to reclaim their connection. Though it did make them more connected, the author admits that at the end of the year she felt "downright ebullient" knowing she didn't have to have sex that day. On the other hand, I recently read a blog post titled "Giving Up On Sex."[2] Here the author and his wife decided to take sex off the table entirely, thereby removing the pressure to have sex, given that their needs were typically not in sync. They both felt a huge sense of relief, and their marriage benefited.

So whether you're having sex every day, or removing it completely from your repertoire, it's clear that sex and kids are not compatible. My friend Kaitlyn recently got divorced. As we discussed the reasons behind her marriage ending, she cited the fact that she and her husband didn't have great chemistry. The sex was not, and never had been, fulfilling. If only she'd known how irrelevant this concern would become if she had kids.

With three children approaching their teens, my preference for Chelsea Handler over *coitus interruptus* is undeniable. As a matter of fact, my desire (or lack thereof) is so strong that I've even supported my husband's girlfriend fantasy. Here's a quick peek into my bedroom on any given evening:

---

1  Charla Muller, *365 Nights: A Memoir of Intimacy*, The Berkley Publishing Group, (2008).

2  John Kinnear, *Giving Up On Sex*, www.askyourdadblog.com (May 15, 2014)

It was 11 o'clock at night and time for my date with Chelsea. After putting all three kids to be myself, I did a quick scan to make sure they had clean clothes for school the next day. My husband was downstairs relaxing on the couch. He doesn't usually participate in the nighttime routine because he claims that reading to the kids hurts his throat. Who cares about his throat? He is not, for the record, an opera singer or radio personality.

I was finally enjoying the day's first minutes to myself. I sat in bed, alone, with the latest issues of *Star* and *People* mounting the top of the pile of clutter next to my bed, just in case I got bored during the commercials. I couldn't wait to read about Kim Kardashian's third fairy-tale wedding.

Knowing my husband most likely fell asleep on the couch, I felt a little guilty. Should I have woken him up and brought him to bed? I looked around the empty room and cherished being alone. This erased all feelings of guilt. The silence of the room was a sharp contrast to the increased volume of the commercials. I turned the volume down so I wouldn't wake him.

Too late. I heard the stairs creak. He was on his way up to the bedroom. He would have that half-asleep, very needy look on his face, expecting sex. Crap! Should I pretend to be asleep? No, I wanted to watch *Chelsea Lately*, and if he comes upstairs he'll put on some show about World War II or that freak who eats bugs and turds. I'll stand my ground.

"Hey, how come you didn't wake me up?" he asked. I ignored him but truthfully I just wanted to be left alone. I wanted to fill my need for self-care. I didn't want to engage in dialogue. I didn't want to shut off the TV. I certainly didn't want to have sex, and I could tell by the look in his eyes that sex is exactly what he was craving.

A few women have told me that they never really liked sex and felt relieved that once they were married with children they didn't have to do it as often, if at all. This was not the case for me. However, these days, sex is the last thing on my mind. Aside from working full-time and caring for our children, I'm also primarily responsible for maintaining the cleanliness of our home. Admittedly I'm not always successful at attaining true cleanliness and my husband actually, on several occasions, has had the audacity to mention my slovenly ways and how I should get more organized. "*Good Housekeeping* called. They want their award back," he teases. Yeah, like that's gonna put me in the mood.

Perhaps I'd be more in the mood if I were married to someone like my friend Pam's husband. He's a stay-at-home dad who not only takes care of the kids and the house, but also caters to her wants and needs. When she gets home from a hard day's work, he hands her a chilled glass of chardonnay and gives her a foot rub. If she so much as boils water for pasta, he praises her endlessly. I, on the other hand, get scolded for spreading the peanut butter too thin when I make the kids' lunches. It should, after all, reach the edge of the crust on all four corners. How did I not know this?

Anyway, he climbed into bed, cozied up to me and tried to get me in the mood. I tightened every muscle in my body and dared not move an inch in hopes he would fall back to sleep. My body remained frigid. Couldn't he see I was exhausted? Didn't the fuzzy red panda pajamas give him the hint? I hoped if I ignored him he would lose interest and eventually fall asleep. Sometimes his persistence pays off and I often relent, with a large sigh. His response: "Jeez, you'd think you just got picked for jury duty."

On this night he got my hint and retreated. "If I were Brad Pitt you'd want to have sex with me." This comment was so ridiculous I didn't even bother responding. I should have told him that if Brad Pitt walked in the room with an armload of freshly laundered and perfectly folded clothes, which he proceeded to place in the correct drawers, then yes, I'd be ready to create the beast with two backs. Otherwise, he too would get rejected.

I recently read a book called *Bad Mother* by Ayelet Waldman. She has admitted publicly that, despite having four children, she and her husband share a vibrant sex life. As a result she's received countless emails from men asking how they can make their wives more like her. She has told them in so many words: just do some laundry. Why don't they get it? My laundry, on the other hand, sat in a pile in the corner of the bedroom. Just staring at it made me angry. It certainly did not make me feel sexy. I rolled over, which seemed to really get his ire up. "I'm going to have to get myself a girlfriend," he said, and with that he fell asleep.

I told my friends about this common late-night scenario. Two of them were horrified and one, a realist, began to help me embrace the idea. "Maybe she'll help you out on Saturdays while he's golfing," she mused. This got me thinking. I'm not a jealous person. Could I handle a mistress? Could I make this work? Could this satisfy both of our needs – his need for more sex, and my need for time to myself?

In my mind's eye I saw her: an energetic, cute, sex-loving twenty-five-year-old with the look of Elle Macpherson and the temperament of Mary Poppins. She could easily morph into either role: sexual plaything or nanny.

I saw him coming home from his romps in a good mood. Moody Daddy be gone! He attempted to get into shape for her, going to the gym, eating healthy food. He looked good. He felt guilty and probably bought me things, sent me off to a spa for the weekend while my kids are with their grandparents so he could be with her. I wondered what spa he'd choose … hopefully a good one. Best of all, each night I was left alone with my buddy Chelsea.

Maybe we'll even separate for a while. He'll go live with her and take the kids every other weekend. Can you imagine? They leave on Friday night and don't return until Sunday night. Every … other … weekend. I'm getting giddy just thinking about it. Maybe she'll even become like a sister-wife and help me out with the kids, tackle some of the housework, give me advice on what's hip and cool so my soon-to-be teens will appreciate me more and I'll no longer be an embarrassment to them. This was starting to sound so appealing that I even thought about going out of my comfort zone and suggesting a threesome, just to get the ball rolling. Or perhaps I could host an old fashioned key party, then hide out in the bathroom with my *Star* and *People* magazines while my husband had sex with someone else's wife. Works for me.

Do I worry that he'll leave us for good? Nah, he's not the type to leave his family and, despite the tone of this story, we actually really enjoy each other. Plus, she'll leave him first. The prospect of endless weekends with his children will be certain death for that relationship. Trust me, I know those kids well. He'll come back to us, eventually returning to his old self, but for a short time we had a fun-loving, attractive, generous, guilty dad/husband. I, on the other hand, got some much-needed help and the bed to myself each night. It was a good run.

Get a girlfriend, he threatened? If only.

# VII. You're Going to Miss These Days!

*By Kim*

Back in my mid-twenties, I went a local winery with my boyfriend. He packed a picnic that we enjoyed on the grass with the bottle of wine we'd just bought. There we sat, basking in the glow of being a young couple in love, enjoying a spectacular day together. Halfway into our bottle of wine, our peaceful afternoon became interrupted by the loud sound of children. I looked over and saw two couples besieged by a gaggle of kids running around, screaming and fighting. The adults all appeared frustrated and annoyed as they tried fruitlessly to convince the children to sit down and eat already. The kids ignored them completely. One of the moms caught my eye and yelled out: "You look happy. Don't ruin your life by having kids!" At the time I was shocked she'd say such a thing in front of her children. Looking back, however, I applaud her honesty.

Now I rarely receive such honesty from those who've gone before me. Instead I am on the receiving end of this all-too-familiar scenario: I'm somewhere in public, having a grand old time trying to wrangle my two boys, ages five and two. It's typically at the supermarket or Target, but it's happened pretty much everywhere. My boys are antagonizing each other, running up and down the aisles, screaming and laughing. I grab them and pull them into the cart. The screaming continues, as does the relentless whining for a toy or candy. We've all been there so I'm sure you can picture the scene. I'm about to blow when some well-meaning douchebag comes up to me and says: "You're going to miss these days. Believe me, you will!"

I stare at this person in disbelief. Is she not seeing what I'm seeing? Look at me – I'm uglier than I was in the '80s. (And who would have thought that was possible?) My face screams exhaustion and misery. Look at my kids – they're animals! This is like a bad scene out of a Jim Carey film. How could I possibly miss these days?

The person typically goes on to tell me how I won't remember all the bad times, only the good. Soon they'll be doing their own thing and I'll be pining for a toddler to snuggle on my lap. When it's put this way, I almost believe it. From a distance it's easy to see why I might miss these days. My boys are adorable and very loving. The older one still showers me with hugs and kisses and is the ultimate mama's boy. The younger one is ridiculously cute and charming. He's outgoing and friendly and laughs out loud at everything. I probably will miss the way he asks for a glass of "wa wa" or how he emulates his older brother by fighting bad guys with a sword, even though he has no clue why. He's unlikely to get cuter so I'm sure I will miss staring at his gorgeous face, admiring his extra-long lashes and the way he runs, especially with a full diaper. OK, I'll bite. I'll miss these days.

As the months tick by, however, I am firmly convinced that in no way, shape or form will I miss these days. As a matter of fact, if I could just bypass ages two through four altogether I gladly would. Let me tell you about a typical day and perhaps by the end my reasoning will be clear.

I wake up bright and early, courtesy of one child or the other. I am not at all rested, thanks to the fact that I slept in bed with my toddler who kicked me all night long and woke up periodically screaming throughout the night. Have you ever been woken by the sound of a small child screaming in your ear? Imagine experiencing that every night, sometimes several times. Forget beauty sleep; I'm just trying to get some "Not too fugly" sleep.

We get up and the relentless request for things begins. It always starts with cheese. For some reason my toddler is obsessed with cheese and must consume it throughout the day, even though it makes him poop like a rabbit. After cheese comes milk, as if the cheese didn't provide enough dairy. Then we move onto the less healthy genre of food: pops, goldfish, gummies, cough drops, vitamins – but only in unreasonable quantities.

Next comes the onslaught of requests to watch TV. These requests are mostly from my five-year-old, but they are nonetheless requests I must deny. I don't deny them because I'm against watching TV – I actually love TV and all things electronic. They have saved my life on many occasions. However, if I turn that TV on first thing in the morning, my kids turn into television zombies, who are quiet and never fight. I therefore enter a state of bliss that I will never voluntarily leave, meaning the TV would stay on all day and night. I know deep down that this is so very wrong that I resist the urge to give in and say no for now. Most days.

Once they've had some breakfast and begin to play, they also begin to fight. I wouldn't care so much about the bumps and bruises and bleeding, but with fights come screaming. From the many nights I've shared a bed with my toddler, I now have a serious case of Post-Traumatic Stress Disorder and I cannot bear the sound of my toddler's scream. Also, if you've ever heard him scream, you would be surprised that he still has vocal cords left, especially knowing that he screams like that all day long, every day. His scream is so lethal that I have been told, on more than one occasion, that he has a future in the horror movie industry. I keep praying his vocal cords will give out, but alas, they're fit as a fiddle.

If we stay home, it's hell. If we go out to do errands, it's double-hell. Plus I will run into some idiot telling me I'll miss these days. The best option is to go somewhere kid-friendly: a playground, the children's museum, an indoor play place, etc. Yay. If you've read Chapter 1, you know how I feel about these activities

Getting ready to leave the house is always a treat. This time it's the five-year-old who's my problem because he once again is ignoring my request to get dressed. I've read umpteen parenting books and tried all the suggestions: letting him do it when he's ready, having a chart of all the things he needs to do before we leave, making him go out in his pajamas because he didn't get dressed, blah, blah, blah. None of them work for long and I still find myself, every single morning, screaming at him to get dressed already. I know this is a sign of my bad parenting, but I'm too tired to care at this point.

Now I have to get ready and my coffee's kicking in. I head to the bathroom to do my business. Inevitably the kids start fighting or they follow me in to ask me to do something for them. When I say "Not now, I'm busy," I'm met with whining and complaining. The sound of a child's whine makes my sphincter close up like a frightened snail. There goes my one chance to clean the pipes.

I leave the house, constipated and un-showered, yet again. Now comes the task of getting both kids in the car. I don't dare even consider buckling in the toddler as we're in the "I do it!" phase. This is the phase where the toddler insists he must do everything himself, even though he sucks at it and it takes forever.

I bite my tongue and wait … and wait … and wait as he fumbles with the buckle and starts to cry in frustration because he can't do it. Of course you can't do it numbskull, you're two! I try to show him what to do but that makes things worse. Now my blood pressure is starting to rise because I know how this ends: I buckle him in and he screams, once again activating my PTSD.

Now we're in the car. Where to go? What to do? Have you tried to find activities that you can do with both a five-year-old and a two-year-old? It's not easy. I cannot bear another minute on a playground … not one more stinking minute. There aren't classes that accommodate both. My older son loves movies and theater. We tried the movies but the two-year-old is ready to leave after about ten minutes. Live theater should be different though, right? It's summer and there's a local children's theater showing *Cinderella*. We drive to the theater, buy our tickets and enter through the big double-doors. I see young kids everywhere; mostly girls in blue dresses, but my boys are not afraid to embrace their inner princess. They allow the kids to sit on the floor in front of the stage, which should prevent any issues we might have of sitting still. I exhale for the first time in over three hours and foolishly think we might experience an enjoyable morning.

Silly woman – what planet are you on, thinking you could take a two-year-old to a play? After Act I, my toddler is done. He gets up and runs around, laughing at my futile attempts to catch him. When I hold him in my lap, he begins screaming. We have to leave the theater while my five-year-old stays behind and watches the play by himself. Lesson learned.

We leave after the play and come home for lunch and a theoretical nap. I say "theoretical" because both of my boys boycotted naps by age two and a half. The only way I could get either of them to sleep was to do "the snooze cruise": drive around for however long it takes for him to fall asleep, then sit in the car and listen to NPR or read a book while he naps. It's a gas guzzler for sure, but worth every ounce of fossil fuel just to get me a break and them some sleep.

Every day comes with a decision: take a snooze cruise so the toddler can get some sleep? Or put on the TV so I can get out of the car and actually get some stuff done? Unfortunately there are only a few shows that hold his attention, and even then I'm looking at an hour at the most. I look at the clock and my heart sinks: two o'clock. Four-plus hours until Daddy gets home. Ugh.

I choose the TV. The boys watch a show and I eat lunch, do laundry, go to the bathroom (finally!) and answer some emails. By this point the toddler is done with TV and ready to play. He's so tired, however, that his play is terrifying. Every train track that doesn't click easily into place enrages him beyond reproach. The screaming continues, sometimes for no reason at all other than the fact that he can scream. He even gives me a look that says "Yeah, I'm screaming. What are you going to do about it, bitch?" Why didn't I choose the snooze cruise? Why, oh why?

At this point in the day I can't go out because he'll fall asleep in the car and I don't want him to nap because he'll be up until 9:30 or 10. By now I have zero tolerance for toddler tantrums. As I sit here and write this, he is screaming in frustration at the fact that he can't put a piece of paper on the fridge with the magnet. Please let this day end already!

Finally Daddy arrives home and I get a brief respite. Then it's the bedtime routine where we have to struggle to get them both to sleep on their own. Inevitably they want one, or both of us, to stay in the room till they fall asleep. If we don't, one or both of them comes down the stairs, exclaiming their fear of zombies or some other fictitious horror. By now I feel physically unable to be in such close proximity with my children; I'm just that done.

We typically succeed in getting them both to sleep by eight. I collapse onto the couch and give my husband the "don't even think about asking for sex" look. He knows not to bother and settles for a mutual foot rub instead. We watch a quick show together then retire to bed, ready to do it all again the next day.

For sure, some days are better and some are worse. In the fall, my older son will start kindergarten and I'll get a respite from the never-ending sibling rivalry. Some of the parenting techniques I'm currently trying to employ will eventually take hold and the screaming will subside; the clothes will get on the body in a reasonable time; the fighting will take place in the basement where I can't witness or hear the mayhem. The problem, however, is that these challenges will be replaced by new, more artful challenges that require more reading, research and resilience.

The bottom line: parenting young children is grueling. I find it to be emotionally, physically and mentally draining and it's just so fucking relentless. Some days I feel like I'm in prison as I am so beholden to my children that I fail to exist. I cannot escape. I get some free time in the yard and the TV room, but mostly I'm locked in my mommy cell where I can never shower or poop in private and I have to work long hours in the mess hall for no pay.

Some days I wonder why I ever wanted to have children in the first place. I feel terrible saying such a thing. It has nothing to do with my kids, but rather my own shortcomings, as I feel so overwhelmed by their otherwise age-appropriate behavior. The fact that I waited until later in life to have kids definitely adds to my dilemma. I lived thirty-eight long years, all of which were about Yours Truly, and Yours Truly alone. I thought I'd be ready to give up that so-called selfish lifestyle, but instead I miss it, sometimes terribly. At a recent trip to Panera with my kids, I saw a young woman sitting alone, sipping a cup of coffee and reading a book. I stared her down, green with envy, practically salivating at the thought of trading places with her, just for that moment in time.

What I miss most is the easy, carefree way in which I went about my day. Having to stop and pick up a few groceries was no big deal. Now, the thought of having to take both of my kids into a grocery store makes my stomach start churning. I won't do it. We've been known to go without milk for days. Sometimes I feel so pathetic – after all, they're so small. Why are they so dang intimidating? Then I recall my baby's tantrums; his loud piercing screams; his brother's constant taunting of him; the whining; the complaining; their constant needs to be changed, fed, bathed, entertained, driven here and there, read to, taught, sung to, stimulated, have their asses wiped. Then I remember why I'm so intimidated: because parenting them never ends. Ever.

I recently had a conversation with a friend who's trying to have a baby. It's taking his wife longer than they expected, so they're discussing their options, which include adoption. I know I felt that same way once, but now it's almost impossible for me to understand this line of thinking: give up your wonderful life full of travel, money and freedom, for *this*?! Then he said something that made it all clear. He began telling me about a visit to his cousin's house. She has two young girls, who are extremely well-behaved. "Angels," he called them, more than once. I knew as he spoke that he's picturing he and his wife having children like that: angels. They won't be like my boys. We all held similar assumptions. The badly behaved children are someone else's problem, but they won't be mine, right?

Wrong. I didn't birth "angels," and looking around, I don't know too many families who did. While they do bring moments of unparalleled joy to our lives, they also add layers of stress and frustration that will disappear when they leave the nest. Will I miss the cute stuff? Sure, but that's what videos and photos are for. Will I miss the rest of it? About as much I miss cold sores, the flu and that case of chlamydia I got in law school. (Don't judge. I got it from my boyfriend.)

Discussing my woes with my friend Karen did not help. As the mother of two adult daughters, she said, "You only dislike toddlers because you have yet to experience teenagers. At least your toddlers are still cute and love you unconditionally. When they're teens, they're a royal pain in the ass and they're often not so cute. The teen years suck!"

So the ugly fact is that, as bad as these days are, they are sheer heaven compared with raising a teenager. I might, if I'm lucky, enjoy a few elementary school years before my older son turns thirteen, grows body hair, has wet dreams and makes my life miserable with his constant scowl and raging hormonal outbursts.

Eventually he'll leave the nest and go to college or get a job. He'll no longer be my little baby, but a grown man who will barely have time to fight with his younger brother or give his mom a hug. My younger son will eventually be gone too and I will be alone again. I will have countless hours to fill with all the things I once loved: yoga, painting, reading, cooking, travel, food shopping in peace. I will reconnect with my husband and maybe have a revival of romance in our relationship. I can go for walks, grow a garden, slow down a bit.

When I then go to the grocery store and see a young mom chasing her toddler, I'm sure my mind will fill with memories of my sons at that sweet, adorable age. I will most likely be tempted to look at her with a smile and say, "You'll miss these days." That is, until her two-year-old lets out a bloodcurdling scream for no apparent reason, thereby activating my PTSD and only one thought will enter my mind: better you than me, honey!

# VIII. FIFTY SHADES OF BLACK AND WHITE, BUT DEFINITELY NOT GRAY.

*By Dawn*

"I want crazy vanilla," she demanded.

"They don't have crazy vanilla," I told her, as I held my breath at the ice cream shop, waiting for my daughter's reaction to my bad news.

"But that's what I want!" she whined.

I informed her again that they don't have crazy vanilla. She could choose plain vanilla (which, by the way, tastes exactly the same as crazy vanilla without the flavorless, colored specks) or frozen lemonade from the truck outside. These choices did not appease her and the tantrum began – crying, yelling and foot-stomping, followed by a complete meltdown as she was unable to make a decision. All eyes were on me and my child as her tantrum was in full swing. There was no stopping it.

If you've ever been around a toddler, this scene most likely sounds all too familiar. The difference here, however, is that my daughter was ten at the time of this tantrum, much too old in the eyes of most adults to be behaving this way. As a result, the stares I received at the ice cream shop that day were not at all sympathetic. They were judgmental – of me as a bad parent and of my daughter as a brat. Little did they know we were neither, but rather the victims of cognitive inflexibility.

Cognitive inflexibility is a psychological disorder in which the afflicted person has difficulty processing more than one possibility at a time. A child with this disorder cannot adjust her thinking in response to any kind of change. When faced with any sort of dilemma, these children become lost and their behavior escalates beyond control. Negotiation with such a child is impossible at the height of the storm. And the worst part – there is no warning that it's about to happen.

Take this example: Last Christmas, I took my daughter and her younger sister to see *The Nutcracker*. She had been looking forward to this outing for weeks. I remember with such clarity hearing her excited little-girl voice poring over the details about the ballet – where she would sit (next to me), what snack she would eat at intermission (chocolate chip cookies), and what souvenir she would buy (a ballerina snow globe).

The day of the ballet finally arrived. After taking our seats, an extremely large person sat in front of my daughter so she was unable to see the stage. I offered her a plethora of options – sit on my lap, raise her own seat with a pile of coats, switch seats to an empty one – nothing I said or did would allay her frustration. She sat there frozen, panic on her face, as she kept saying "no" to all of my suggestions.

The tantrum escalated to the point that we had to leave our seats. We ended up watching much of the performance in the lobby on the small, distorted black-and-white TV. I envisioned other parents having to suffer through unruly behavior and being relegated to the foyer. How did this happen when she was so excited to be here? Though the thought of grabbing my daughter by the hair and dragging her to the car entered my mind, I knew I couldn't leave because we'd driven with another family who expected a ride home from us. Plus, my younger daughter was still enjoying the ballet.

I was positively seething with anger while my child's tantrum continued. I couldn't leave the lobby and I couldn't reenter the theater. I was her captive. All that money and effort spent on tickets for nothing; we could have stayed home and watched *The Nutcracker* on a much nicer TV. I kept trying to breathe in – 1, 2, 3 – and out – 4, 5, 6. I felt condescending stares from the blue-and-white-haired ushers. "What are you looking at, you old bat?" I thought to myself, even though I knew exactly what they were looking at: a young child completely out of control. My daughter, unfazed, continued her moaning and groaning.

At one point she called me a jackass. It's one thing to think of the word "jackass" in reference to one's mother. Verbalizing those thoughts is a whole different ball of wax. The scene gave the impression that swearing was part of my daughter's vocabulary (untrue), and my credibility as a parent and a human being was going downhill fast. I prayed to be swallowed up by the floor, but it didn't happen. My anger swelled even more, yet I knew, just like the dancers, I had an audience, so I maintained my cool. In my head, though, the thoughts started to swirl: could I leave her here and run away? If I smacked her in the head and knocked her unconscious, for how long would I go to jail? Would jail be better than this?

Then, in an instant, everything changed. It was as if a switch went off; she was ready to go back in the theater. There was absolutely no transition – just irrational to rational. Dumbfounded, physically drained and emotionally numb, I followed her back in and took a seat. Merry fucking Christmas.

I don't always maintain my cool so well. Last spring, I took the kids to the zoo. Being school vacation, the zoo was ridiculously busy, so we had to park what felt like two miles from the entrance. The weather was iffy, so I suggested to my daughter that she bring her fleece jacket. She couldn't decide whether to take the jacket because she didn't want to carry it if she got too warm. To stave off a major tantrum, I made an executive decision to leave the jacket in the car and began walking to the zoo entrance. A few paces from the car and she changed her mind; she wanted the jacket. I breathed in, turned around, and grabbed the jacket as we once again headed toward the entrance. She dragged the jacket on the ground, moaning about carrying it and demanding that I bring it back to the car.

Something about watching her treat her North Face fleece like an old rag made the tension, which had previously been bubbling below the surface, begin to mount with uncontrollable force. At last Mount Vesuvius erupted. I grabbed the jacket from her and began furiously swatting her with the fleece, yelling and screaming like a crazy person. I would have continued my rant but feared that someone was taping me on their cell phone and I'd later appear on YouTube. At least I'd be known as the mom who beats her daughter kindly, using only the softest of materials, right?

I knew that I had to regain control or she would repeat these episodes for the rest of the day. "That's it, you owe me 15 minutes!" This is a technique our doctor suggested and it is surprisingly effective. Basically, when she wastes my time with a tantrum or unreasonable behavior, she owes me that time. It's taken away from an activity that she likes to do. However, I couldn't add time for the comments my daughter would make under her breath. If I did, it would leave her in a permanent stage of vegetation. Not that I'd be complaining at this point …

We walked through the zoo in search of a picnic spot while my daughter continued her breathy snide comments and I tried my best to ignore them. Eventually we found a place to eat lunch – a task that should involve no drama. Alas, my daughter didn't want the sandwich I bought for her. She didn't know what she wanted. She only knew what she didn't want – what I was offering. She sat there with a puss on her face and continued to grunt like a wild animal. My oldest child looked at me and asked, "Is this going in the book?"

"Yes indeed," I thought to myself. "Yes indeed."

Anyway, it happened again – the switch went off and she changed. She asked for her sandwich and began eating. The wild animal disappeared, replaced by my sweet, beautiful girl. I sat there, every nerve on edge, still feeling the effects of her horrendous behavior, while she peacefully munched on her turkey sandwich. I'm not sure who needs medication more: my daughter or me.

In all fairness to my child, the behavior she exhibits isn't entirely her fault, nor is it mine (despite the many comments I hear, either to my face or behind my back, that she has some serious discipline problems). Having been blessed with cognitive inflexibility, she lives in the realm of black and white – there can be no gray. Offering her good choices or alternatives only causes her to get more anxious. She flourishes in a concrete world, a world of absolutes. We were either going or we weren't. She could have it or she couldn't. Sarah's doctor explained that it was better to just say "no" rather than "I don't know" or "maybe." As the parent I could exercise my right to change my mind at a later time. Who knew parents had rights?

I always thought that giving my daughter choice would empower her. After all, every parenting book I'd ever read mandated that we give our children choice. Do you want ice cream or lemonade? Do you prefer this seat or that one? Should you bring your fleece or leave it in the car? Instead, I left the poor kid in a complete state of angst every time I forced her to choose one thing over another. By trying hard to be a good parent, I was unknowingly causing my daughter more stress.

After my daughter's diagnosis, I turned to the Internet for some answers. There, I sadly learned that due to cognitive inflexibility, she would be at risk for anorexia nervosa, obsessive-compulsive disorder, schizophrenia and autism. ADHD was also on the list, but that diagnosis was already confirmed – check. Next I reflected on obsessive-compulsive disorder, aka OCD. My mind immediately filled with images of my daughter's Barbie dolls arranged manically in order like little logs, side by side. OCD – check? Then I thought of her meager appetite and pictured her small, thin body. Anorexia nervosa – check? How about those mood swings and seemingly split personality? Schizophrenia – check? ADHD is one thing, but what are talking about here? Images of my daughter wearing tin foil on her head and speaking with aliens paralyzed me.

I asked her doctor if these diagnoses were possible. She cautiously responded, "We'll see. It's too early to tell." That's not the answer I wanted to hear. Like my daughter, in this case I needed a clear, absolute answer. "We'll see" was unsettling, as it meant there was a chance she would be mentally unstable. Imagining my daughter living with serious mental illness, unable to hold a job or maintain a romantic relationship devastated me. I cannot accept such a fate for my child and have committed to do anything it takes to help her become a fully functioning adult.

As I continued to search for answers, I found video games could be helpful as they increased mental flexibility. Call of Duty, Grand Theft Auto, whatever it takes – violence, nudity and inappropriate language become irrelevant when you're talking about the difference between a normal future and a not-so-normal one. This goes against everything I've ever learned, but everything I've ever learned hasn't done shit for me where this child is concerned.

The good news is that most children outgrow this affliction as their frontal lobe develops – something that typically happens by age twenty-five. That gives me fifteen years, more or less, to worry about her fate – fifteen long, but short, years. I pray that my daughter will develop normally and avoid the more serious disorders associated with cognitive inflexibility.

In the meantime, however, I feel compelled to wear a sign that says, "It's not my fault! My kid has cognitive inflexibility!" I'm tired of the stares and accusations. Whether to blame or not, I look like a schmuck to everyone around me.

Luckily there are a few friends who are aware of my situation and provide me with the support and validation I so desperately need. Remember the ice cream situation? I happened to be at the ice cream shop with one of those friends. She watched my child struggle with her decision: to defer instant gratification and get frozen lemonade later or get the lowly, plain vanilla. She saw the angst on the young girl's face as she refused to consider the two options and instead decided to simply complain about the lack of crazy vanilla. I wanted to dunk her entire head, upside down, into the vat of ice cream. Society – and the large glass counter – prevented me from doing so.

Instead I waited out the storm, stayed firm and calm and said, "That's enough. You're going to owe me time." The switch went off, she stopped her tantrum, and she opted for ice cream. Later, she even apologized saying, "Mommy, I'm sorry for giving you so much trouble about the ice cream." I looked at her dumbfounded – who are you and what have you done with my irrational child? No matter, she's in a better place, but what about me?

After the ice cream episode, my friend told me that I handled the situation with amazing grace and patience. "I don't know what I would have done," she mused. "Probably dragged her out of there by the hair, telling her ice cream was no longer an option. But that's not fair to do to a kid like her. She's lucky to have you as her mom."

I felt a mix of relief and pride. Maybe I'm not so bad at this after all. Maybe the world doesn't see me as a terrible parent who can't control her child. Who knows? Either way, I'll take each storm as it comes, and try, in the meantime, to stay off YouTube.

# IX. FORGET THE COLLEGE FUND AND SAVE FOR THERAPY.

*By Kim*

In my mid-thirties I had already managed to destroy one marriage and was slowly killing a good relationship with a good, stable man, thanks to my inability to maintain a level of cool when things didn't go my way. I had been in therapy for quite a while, dealing with the truly big issues but decided it was time to go further – time to become a better person and have a shot at a real, adult relationship (to the extent that they exist).

I asked for an emergency session after a particularly bad fight with my then-boyfriend, now husband, during which he decided to leave rather than fight with me. I couldn't imagine why because I put up a really good fight, and who would want to miss out on that? He did, apparently, and out the door he went and into his car. My heart became tight in my chest and started racing as my breath became shallow and panic set in. "He left me? How dare he! Who does he think he is? I'll show him!" And so the mania began as I ran out the front door with no coat. This only highlighted my insanity because it was January in Boston and way too cold to be outside without a coat, unless you had mental health issues. Apparently I did, as chasing a car any time of the year isn't exactly a sign of good mental health.

Did I expect to actually catch up to him? If I did catch dumb luck in the form of traffic lights, what would I do when I reached his car? These are not questions I actually wanted to answer because I failed to have a rational thought at this point. Yet on I went until I realized he was gone. So I went back home and frantically dialed his cell phone for the next twenty minutes until I exasperated him completely and he agreed to come back and continue the fight. I cannot recall the subject of the fight, but I definitely remember my feelings when he left: helpless, scared and abandoned.

I relayed this to my therapist who politely jotted down notes in her notebook and looked at me without reproach, even though I feared my lack of real problems bored her, or worse, that my immaturity managed to horrify even a seasoned professional. She looked up at me over her glasses.

"This sounds like a classic case of abandonment. Something happened to you, and your parents weren't there for you, creating a fear of abandonment in your adult relationships. You may not recall what happened and it's not important, since it could be as simple as being left in your crib to cry as a baby. What's important is that you learn to cope."

I sat there stunned. I couldn't believe that something so normal as leaving a baby to cry in her crib could cause such damage as an adult. Now at the time I did not have children, nor did I really think about having them, so I had never heard of Dr. Ferber, or such books as *Healthy Sleeping Habits, Happy Child* or *The No Cry Sleep Solution*. I didn't know this was a real dilemma for parents. Being born in the late '60s to parents who were not hippies meant I was a proud, healthy, formula-fed baby who slept on her tummy, hung out in her walker and watched *Sesame Street* and soap operas for hours on end before I could even talk. When I became a colicky pain in the ass, my pediatrician prescribed "fuss pills." I shouldn't really say "prescribed" because he simply put them in a little white envelope and handed them to my mother. To this day she has no idea what they were, but she did say they eradicated my pain in the ass-ness. Admittedly I was a tad hyper as a child, but I attributed this to the fact that my mother took speed when she was pregnant with me, prescribed by her doctor because she was gaining too much weight. Man I miss the '60s! These, I assume, came in the form of an actual prescription known as amphetamines, unlike those fuss pills. All of this created amusing fodder for the dinner table later in life, but I never considered it a problem because I was fine. All of us turned out just fine, right?

I can now safely say that chasing your boyfriend's Volvo down the street in the dead of winter is not "fine." On some level it seems quite disturbing, so when I decided to have children I knew one thing they would not suffer at my hands: abandonment. I would be the picture of attachment parenting. I would nurse my babies until my nipples fell off. I would allow them to sleep in my bed as long as necessary. I would wear my babies in a sling or wrap while I did housework or went for a walk. My children would not end up in therapy, hearing that they suffered from abandonment issues. No way.

When my first son was born I lived up to my word. If he so much as uttered a tiny cry, I went flying to his room and picked him up. I held him for naps and nursed him to sleep every night. When he rejected his crib, I happily put him between my husband and me, creating a gap that still exists five-plus years later courtesy of my second son, who equally hates his crib. I never let him cry for more than a few seconds at a time.

My son was a horrid sleeper, and I complained about my exhaustion often to my fellow playgroup moms, which is how I learned about Dr. Ferber and other sleep trainers. I read all the books and they had me sold until the part where they talked about letting your baby "cry it out." I refused, and instead became a martyr for the cause. I felt smugly superior at playgroups for being the only mom who wouldn't let her baby cry himself to sleep. I hadn't had a full night's sleep since before he was born and I was proud of it. I basked in the knowledge that their daughters would be chasing my son down the street, and not the opposite.

Being at the beck and call of an infant, however, is no simple task. It's not just the physical exhaustion, but also the fatigue of trying to defend one's actions to those who parented in the '70s or '80s, or who parent today with a more mainstream style. Sometimes I felt crazy – was I the only one who wouldn't let her child cry? Chasing a car on foot in the dead of winter aside, I felt rather sane. Also, my choices felt like the right ones for me, so I turned to the natural parenting magazines and mother-earth bloggers for some support.

*Mothering* was my favorite magazine during pregnancy, as I loved the photos of those gorgeous babies wrapped in neutral-colored organic blankets, gazing up at their mother's faces while they nursed. Based on much I'd read there, I chose to birth naturally with a midwife, use cloth diapers and breastfeed for at least year. Little did I know at the time that these decisions would provide me an all-access pass to the Attachment Parenting Club. My fellow playgroup moms must have suspected I was a member of that Club, as they accused me of also being a vegetarian (I am not) and often scanned my armpits for excessive hair (which I do not have ... most of the time).

Being in the Club is the perfect panacea when you're looking for validation for your actions. It's great fun to peruse the discussion boards where like-minded women go to offer support, get advice, and bash others who – God forbid – push their babies in a stroller instead of wearing them in a sling. When you read that circumcision is akin to genital mutilation, you pat yourself on the back for leaving your son's foreskin intact.   You nod along about the ease of making your own organic baby food, as opposed to buying those lazy, unhealthy options offered by Gerber. It's nice to be in the Club ... until you realize that Club feels more like a nasty sorority: exclusive, judgmental and reeking of patchouli oil.

The more I read, the more I began to realize that bonding over one's similarities is not necessarily the healthiest choice. Pack-mentality begins to develop, as does a mindset of "Us vs. Them." I've never been the sorority-type and have always prided myself on being a live and let live kind of person. Why then, was I turning into the type of woman I despised, simply because I'd birthed a human?

I received my wake-up call when my son was two and a half. That summer, we flew back east to visit family. We got the rental car, visited the in-laws, ate some lunch and retired to my cousin's house where we would be spending the next two weeks. It had been a long day and my little guy, who never napped, fell asleep in the car. I didn't want to wake him, so I left him asleep in his car seat. I was no more than twenty feet away. We had the door open so I could see him the whole time and hear him if he woke, or so I thought.

As happens when family gets together, my cousin and I started chatting and laughing and I completely forgot about my offspring asleep outside. After about a half hour I realized that I hadn't given him a moment's glance in quite some time, so I went outside to check on him.

At this point he was crying so hard that he no longer had a voice, hence the fact that I didn't hear him crying. I have no idea how long he'd been crying, I only knew that he woke up in a strange car in a strange yard, his parents were gone and no matter how hard he cried no one came to rescue him. He was angry at me and didn't even want me to hold him. I knew exactly how he felt: angry, scared, abandoned. This felt all too familiar. Two and a half fucking years of hard work down the drain.

Eventually he got over it and he seems OK, though only his future girlfriends will know for sure. At five, my son is a fantastic sleeper so I don't second-guess my choice to not follow Dr. Ferber. I have simply stopped judging those who do. I realized that no matter how hard we try to protect our children from something, we will screw them up in ways we never even imagined, so get over it. This is strangely comforting to me. Now if only I could land some of those fuss pills.

# X. Choose Wisely.

*By Dawn*

"Choose wisely," I tell my girls. At ages nine and eleven, they assume I'm talking about the style of backpack they'll select for the new school year. Little do they know, however, my desire for them to choose wisely goes much, much deeper.

I stumbled upon my future husband one late summer afternoon at a friend's cookout on Plum Island, a gorgeous remote beach north of Boston. We were all on the beach throwing around a football. I began to wonder if he was attracted to me when he repeatedly threw me a pass. I became intrigued by his tall, athletic build and white 1970s tube socks. Others saw the chemistry and we were set up on our first date. He was my first, and so far my last, love.

We made an ideal couple. My husband, the Alpha Male, fell in love with my innocence and quiet nature. I fell in love with his quick wit and charm. Since I never possessed a jealous streak, his endless jokes about other women, trips to Vegas casinos or guys' golf outings didn't faze me. In turn, I was free to pursue my interests in shopping, ballet and theater. He's also an amazing cook while I, at age forty-six, have just mastered making scrambled eggs. Thrilled to marry someone who'd take over that domestic duty, I felt perfectly matched. We worked well together, like peanut butter and Fluff ... until we had kids.

I have since morphed from Fluff into mayonnaise, which does not mesh well with peanut butter. Don't get me wrong. I still love my husband. It's just that those personality differences that worked so well before children have resulted in an unfortunate level of inequality. No one wants to be mayonnaise. Shall we take a look?

Once the air has a touch of warmth and the ground is no longer covered with snow, golf season begins. This means that each Wednesday, Saturday and often Sundays, my husband plays golf. Whether it's to practice chipping and putting, to compete in a two- or three-day tournament, or to simply play a round, my husband can be found at his beloved club while I'm stuck playing taxi driver to my three children.

As much as I detest having to rush the kids out of the house on a Saturday morning, I find the alternative unbearable. So each week I bring my cherubs to a variety of activities, starting with music lessons. The lessons themselves are uneventful – it's the getting there that kills me. We're always running late. Always. After calmly asking my kids to get ready about twenty-five times, my inner crazy woman is unleashed as I come down the stairs only to see of my nine-year-old daughter sitting at the table, watching a Justin Beiber video … in her pajamas. I glance at the clock. We have less than twenty minutes to get to a place that is twenty-five minutes away. My husband suggests getting them up earlier. I harken back to this brilliant advice that he extols as he walks out the door in a hurry to make his tee time. The advice wasn't helpful then, and certainly is not helpful now.

As I rush around, I picture myself on some reality show, praying that if I can only get to music on time, I'll get immunity from the next challenge: the dreaded bedtime routine. Sometimes I stop and picture what my husband is doing, for the fourteenth Saturday in a row. While I'm stuck in my car, trying to reason with my kids that NPR is more interesting than the top forty countdown, I see him at the first tee, squinting against the glare of the summer sun as he yells "Fore!"

Later as I'm rushing into the local bakery for a calzone, car running with the kids in the back seat, I picture him at the ninth hole, stopping the cart girl for an Arnold Palmer. No alcohol yet as he doesn't want to mess with his game. On the other hand, my 9 a.m. Dunkin' Donuts regular has become pitifully cold. We arrive home for lunch, where, between bites of my calzone, I break up fights and respond to demands – more calzone, more milk, more entertainment, more pieces of my life being sucked out of me. At this point in the day, my husband hits the nineteenth hole, where an array of delicious food and beverage await him. He's smiling, relaxed, happy. He's enjoyed a fun, carefree day. I have not. I'm exhausted and resentful. Then I remember that sweet thing called karma and I imagine him getting hit in the nuts by a stray golf ball. This image puts a slight grin on my face for the first time that day.

When my husband comes home from his day on the course, he too is exhausted. He collapses onto the couch to watch more golf. As I stand there looking at his tired form, I picture that ghostly knight from *Indiana Jones and the Last Crusade* and mutter under my breath, "You chose ... poorly."

My blood starts to boil at the injustice. How, in good conscience, can he lay there watching golf when he knows I've been with the kids all day? Doesn't he pine to give me a break? He assumes that, because he's home, I can be off duty. He, however, will assuredly fall asleep in front of the TV and, if awoken by the kids' fights, he will scream at them to shut up already and fall back asleep. In other words, if I'm off duty, no one's is in charge. This doesn't work for my kids.

I've spoken to other women and it seems that all men are the same. Maybe not to the extreme of my husband, but equally clueless about how much work it takes to run a household and raise children. Most women complain about the distribution of housework. The complaints are the same – whether the woman works or stays home, she's expected to do the lion's share. It's not because all men are selfish and/or slobs. I think women – the gatherers – are born to multi-task, while men – the hunters – are born to provide. Once they've finished their hunt (or golf game), it's time to relax. The gatherer's work, however, is never finished – and therein lies the problem.

In most situations, the woman yells at or cajoles the man. A fight ensues, after which the man, with good intentions, does a load of laundry. Things get better, at least until the next time the woman comes home after a long day at work to find the man lying on the couch while the kids are playing video games and the house looks like a bomb went off. And so it goes …

Our situation is slightly different as I'm not very good at yelling or cajoling. I've tried telling my husband that I'm over-whelmed and need him to take on more responsibilities. He responded by calling me a complainer. I'm not sure what else I can do, as you can't control another person's behavior. I can't change overnight; even if I tried screaming at him, he'd probably laugh at my futile attempts to be controlling. I have nothing. I'm like a British cop who doesn't carry a gun. "Stop or I'll … say 'stop' again." Not very convincing, am I?

Recently I told my friend Sherri about my Saturdays from hell. When I got to the part about the TV golf, she told me in no uncertain terms that she wouldn't put up with it. "What would you do?" I asked innocently enough. "Throw that fucking TV out the window" she said, and she wasn't joking. When I relayed this conversation to another friend, she thought that solution sounded extreme, but agreed that hiding the remote or removing the cable box might be a kinder, gentler option.

Upon reflection, I realize it's not me, but rather the dynamic in our relationship that became solidified over twenty years ago. My husband still lives in the time before children. I know other women similarly situated and it's a problem with no simple cure. My friend Laura is married to someone we'll call "The Renaissance Man." He surfs, snowboards, plays the bongos in a band, makes his own beer and engages in more activities than most sixteen-year-olds. Before they had kids, I envied their fun lifestyle. They had grand parties at their house on what seemed like a weekly basis. Every time we got together, she shared photos of yet another vacation. Life with the Renaissance Man was good, that is until their daughter came along.

Since then, life for Laura has become that of a typical working mother of two – one pint-sized and one fully grown. Life for the Renaissance Man, however, hasn't changed much at all, other than the fact that he now has another member of the family with whom he can play. When my friend insists they leave a party by eight o'clock to put their daughter to bed, the Renaissance Man says to her, "You need to learn to relax and have more fun." When she's short-tempered with their daughter or she complains about her behavior, his response is less than sympathetic: "What's the problem? I think she's easy." "Of course she's easy," she tells me. "She's doing whatever she pleases while he's on his phone, texting or updating his Facebook page." Their relationship, previously free of fighting, is now what seems like a never-ending battle.

Perhaps if we both had an excellent support system, we would need less support from our spouse. Before having kids I'd heard the infamous saying, "It takes a village to raise a child." Although

I found the saying quite powerful, I never fully understood its true meaning. Thirteen years later, it's all too clear. In a village, you're never alone. Scores of family members and fellow villagers act as second parents. No one had to ask for help. Supporting one another was a given, as every village member was involved in the collective raising of all children.

In our modern-day, more isolated society, most of us are doing this alone and the demands of parenting have increased exponentially, particularly when it comes to our children's schedules. Every parent of school-aged children has referred to themselves, at one time or another, as a "glorified taxi." If you have school-aged children, you know exactly what I mean.

This problem is so pervasive that hordes of products have been created to help parents coordinate their children's schedules: cell phone apps, complicated spreadsheets, calendars that cover an entire refrigerator and/or kitchen wall. Parents are syncing their calendars with one another and bargaining with neighbors to carpool or catch a ride. Carting your children to and fro has become a full-time job, not leaving much time for everything else – hence the need for help. More than ever we need our village, yet the village doesn't exist. Instead we are parenting alone, getting help from others only when we are desperate enough to ask.

The first place most of us turn to is family. Like many facets of modern parenting, I had no idea how important a role my parents would play. They have helped me since the moment my first son was born, organizing day-care pick-ups when my husband and I couldn't get there on time and providing me with company when I was at my loneliest. After many years of helping me, they have finally let me know that they have limitations. They "didn't retire to babysit." Seventy is the new fifty, so they're living their lives, like many modern-day grandparents.

I have no siblings on whom to rely. My husband has two sisters and a brother – all of whom live out of state. My husband's mother, well, that's a whole other book.

With my immediate circle depleted or unwilling, I often have nowhere to turn, so I look to friends and parents in my community. Thankfully I am surrounded by wonderful, generous people who are always willing to give my son a ride home from cross country practice or let my daughter spend the night. Nonetheless, I feel like I wear a scarlet letter. Certainly not an "A" – who has the time or desire for an affair? No, I wear a "B" for "burden." I am a burden to everyone around me – a big fat pain in the ass. I imagine that people see me coming, or recognize my name on their caller ID and they want to run and hide. I don't know this for certain, but I'm guessing it because I feel like I'm constantly asking someone to help with my kids, and I hate it.

My current situation cannot easily be changed. I'm a bit of a lost cause. What I can do, however, is offer a few words of wisdom for my fellow sisters.

If you're thinking of having kids, take a look at your village. If your husband plays golf, or is a Renaissance Man, or a man-child in any way, make sure he understands that life will need to change, drastically, once the baby's born. Talk out the details and be clear about your expectations. Maybe even get them in writing. You can't do this alone.

Are your parents or in-laws helpful? What are they willing to do? If they burn out, what's your back-up plan?

If your husband isn't willing to change his ways and help from the future grandparents doesn't look too promising, I'm not suggesting that you forego having children. Just know what you're getting yourself into. Build a village and be prepared to use it. You will need to rely on friends, neighbors, siblings, cousins, aunts, uncles — anyone who is ready, willing and able to be an occasional stand-in parent. You cannot be afraid to ask for, and accept help.

If all else fails, pray you win the lottery. Then you can hire an actual taxi to drive your kids around.

# CONCLUSION

After going through the process of writing and sharing the stories you just read, three secrets to happier parenting revealed themselves to us: friendship, honesty and self-care. Though each of these ingredients is essential to a more gratifying parenting experience, incorporating them into our lives presents some real challenges.

**FRIENDSHIP: Spend more time in the company of women you enjoy -- real women, not online friends.**

In both our conversations with fellow mothers and our research online, as well as our own experience, it's clear that women need to feel connected to one another. Most of us, whether we love parenthood or struggle with it, want to feel understood, without judgment. We desire a symbiotic relationship where we offer support to one another, and receive it in kind. There's nothing better than hearing a conversation or reading a story and saying, "Yes! Someone else feels the same way!"

We know it's not always easy to find other moms with whom we're comfortable sharing our parenting realities. True, there are many avenues to meet one another, especially when you have a new baby: breastfeeding support groups, playgroups, mommy and me classes, etc. We, along with other women we've spoken with, attended these groups with mixed results. While some of us made lifelong friends, many had the opposite reaction. We felt the condescending stares at our cheap pleather shoes and disheveled hair. We felt judged because our babies weren't eating enough or sleeping through the night. We noticed cliques developing and felt shunned if we didn't agree with the majority. Did anyone else share our struggles? If so, they certainly didn't admit to them. It was like reliving junior high all over again.

When support groups and fellow moms fail us, we turn to the mommy blogs. Their names alone draw us in: "Because Motherhood Sucks," "Scary Mommy" and "Motherhood, WTF?" The writers are often telling hilarious, frank stories to which we can most definitely relate. While that's a great place for your quick fix, these online support networks aren't real. These bloggers and commenters are your virtual friends, but the friendship ends on the computer. You can't call them up when you need a hug. You can't have a virtual play date.

Also, you might end up feeling worse about yourself, especially if you dare to glance at the comments. Many women (dubbed "sancti-mommies), and even a fair share of men feel some unexplainable need to write scathing criticisms of each blog entry posted, no matter how benign. One recent example comes to mind – a blog post in which the author advocated inviting friends to your home without feeling the need to put away all the toys and make everything perfect. She posted photos of her lovely living room, scattered with toys and games, looking messy, but not slovenly. This post resonated with us, as it promoted friendship over the façade of perfection. Many readers felt the same way, as evidenced by the most of the comments. Some, however, were downright nasty, criticizing everything from her "lazy" philosophy to the way she decorated her home. Seriously???

This is not a healthy venue for women who are already feeling lonely and insecure. It's too easy to be critical of other's thoughts and actions online, where you're completely anonymous. When you connect with someone in real life, criticizing her actions or opinions is a lot harder to do. When we are in the company of friends, our goal is typically to support and nurture one another. Our online community is not always so well-intentioned, and at times can be unequivocally cruel. True, online friends can be found with the simple click of a mouse, making them a very convenient outlet. We should, however, focus on our energy on those friendships that don't rely on rechargeable batteries or a CPU. We need real, live friends, but how do we make and cultivate new friendships?

**HONESTY: Be honest about your feelings of motherhood, to others and yourself.**

We want to be truthful about motherhood but sometimes our feelings can be so dark we don't even want to admit them to ourselves. If we're truly honest, will we be judged? What if someone tells us a story that shocks our conscience? Can we put on a good poker face?

Aside from the ones we've cited in our stories, here's another great example of the importance of authenticity: During one of our focus groups, Gail admitted that on her recent trip to Arizona she thought, for a millisecond, about throwing her three-year-old into the Grand Canyon and running away, claiming she fell.

We'll admit that even we found this statement shocking. As we listened to Gail talk, however, we were able to see the whole picture. We knew she would never act on that one thought. She told us her story in jest, as a way to convey how difficult she finds child rearing. We were honored that she felt so comfortable telling us about her darkest parenting moments. Most of us have had them and they're impossible to admit to ourselves, never mind to a group of women, many of whom were strangers.

The upside is that, after our focus group, Gail felt understood. She experienced less guilt and more support. Can you imagine the blowback Gail would have suffered if she posted those feelings online? She most likely would have been on the receiving end of countless insults, or worse, reported to Child Protective Services because someone took her a tad too seriously.

The biggest challenge many of us face is determining whether a fellow-mom or new friend is the type of person to whom you can say anything. If you put yourself out there and say how you really feel, how will it be received? Will you become a pariah in your social circle for speaking freely?

**SELF-CARE: Finally, make your own self-care a top priority, or at least on par with needs of the rest of your family.**

We've all been told to engage in self-care. "You're no good for your kids if you're an empty vessel!" Now we feel the pressure to take care of ourselves: an impossible feat for most of us who are already stretched way too thin. When we finally do get a few hours to go shopping, hit the gym or take a walk, it feels like a mere quick fix. After resuming life with children, we are depleted once again within a matter of minutes. We then become like junkies looking for our next high. "Hey, can you give me ten minutes? I just need ten minutes to myself. Please, I'll do anything!"

With no time to engage in *true* self-care, we often turn to the Internet. We check out Pinterest and Facebook, where our guilty consciences are further burdened because we served store-bought cake at our kid's birthday party, or our family vacation didn't create photos worthy of even one Facebook post. So we return to the mommy blogs, because it seems to be the only place women are willing to be authentic. But, as we discussed earlier, this might not be the best self-care solution. What now?

We talked about this conundrum in our focus groups, and most everyone agreed that their needs took a backseat to the needs of their families. One friend pined to just go to a weekly yoga class. The irony, she admitted, is that if her child's doctor recommended weekly yoga, she'd have her child there – each week. When it came to herself, however, she just couldn't make it happen.

We can no longer deny the importance of taking care of ourselves. We all know we're better parents and happier people when we feel like our needs are met. We must make self-care a priority, but how? And where will we find the time?

These "secrets" to happier parenting are nothing of the sort, actually. We've all read articles and books that espouse these same messages in one form or another. We read along, nodding our heads and promising to put the advice into action. The problem, however, is taking that next step, which seems daunting and unattainable. Once we turn away from the computer or close the book, the advice goes to the back of our over-burdened brains, only to become something else we feel guilty for not achieving.

We want to make it easy to take that next step, as the current state of parenting must be scaled back. We can't speak for all of you, but modern-day parenting has taken a toll on us. Aside from feeling overwhelmed and stressed, we've personally experienced a dizzying array of emotions: embarrassment by our public displays of inadequacy, shame at wanting to run away from our kids, weakness for not being able to handle such a simple task as child-rearing. The cost of modern-day parenthood is one we're no longer willing to pay.

So what's the solution?

Throughout the course of this book we've made many comparisons to parenting "back in the day," i.e., the 1970s. Though certainly not perfect, there are a few lessons we could learn from our mothers. The lack of computers in their lives forced them to have telephone or in-person conversations with other women. The absence of parenting books and social media meant less guilt and competition with one another. The absence of guilt allowed them time to freely use sitters and engage in self-care, even it that just meant watching soap operas.

We're not advocating a return to the '70s, but maybe we could all just take a step back in time – extract all the good stuff from our 1970s counterparts and not be so into our children. As we explained in the introduction, we're calling this new mindset "conscious unparenting™." Though we're assuredly poking fun at celebrity elitism, we can't help but admit that the term fittingly describes what we're trying to achieve: an intentional yet mindful step back from all-consuming parenthood toward a more balanced approach.

This is not a one-size-fits-all system; it's about comfortably finding the places where you can cut back and/or make changes, and committing to making it happen. It's about taking some portion of the time you spend on your kids and redirecting it to your own self-care. It's being a bit more of a '70s mom, with a modern-day twist.

Since writing this book, we've tried to put this philosophy into action. For the two of us, our biggest challenges are probably no secret. Kim has been plagued by isolation and boredom, while Dawn's struggled with being overwhelmed yet maintaining false pretenses that everything's OK. One of the things we've found most helpful is to take regularly scheduled time away from our families.

With the help of a few high school friends, we've committed to going away for a weekend twice a year. We spend 24 to 48 hours in the company of people with whom we are completely ourselves. We bare it all to each other and leave feeling validated, understood, and loved. It's expensive and sometimes difficult to schedule, but we're making it work. This time away from our families and the memories we make with great friends is enough to fill our empty vessels time and time again. And better yet, it satisfies our triad of happier parenting.

This might not be the ideal solution for you. Maybe you can't get away for a weekend. Maybe you don't want to be away from your families. Regardless, you can find something similar that helps you fill your vessel and satisfy your needs. Find what works for you and commit to making it happen.

Here's a great example our friend Susy shared. After reading our book, she realized that most family activities in which she engaged were all about the kids: let's go to a kid movie, walk around the mall and shop for kids' clothes, grab dinner at a kid-friendly restaurant. Her daughter is now old enough to understand negotiation, so Susy's decided that family activities will be pleasing to both the child *and* the adult. She put this into practice last weekend, when taking her daughter to a Halloween Party. After a dreadfully boring party replete with bad costumes and a lame magician, a group of friends decided to hit the local creamery for burgers and milkshakes. Susy, however, wanted an adult meal with an adult beverage, so, thinking of our book she said "no," despite the complaints of her daughter. Instead she corralled a few moms to take the party to a local brewery/restaurant. Her daughter was happy enough to be with a close-knit group of friends, and Susy experienced an enjoyable night out. It worked!

Keep in mind, the women you spend time with need not be women who necessarily think and feel like you do about mother-hood. The point of this movement is not to connect only laissez-faire parents, so we can drink wine while we mock the helicopters. Some of our best friends are self-proclaimed helicopter parents and we love them dearly. The point is to cultivate healthy relationships with one another in which we acknowledge and accept our differences. We do this in most other aspects of our lives: some of us live for designer handbags while others prefer to shop at Target. Some like yoga, others prefer running, yet we still manage to be friends.

When it comes to parenting, however, we take our preferences much more personally. We measure our parenting styles against those of others – "I'm not as lackadaisical as that mom!" "They're much more authoritarian than we are!" Like our preferences for purses and exercise, our parenting differences should be celebrated rather than treated with disdain. Once judgment disappears, it's a lot easier to be honest about your thoughts and feelings.

The key to having great relationships with your fellow moms is by showing them you're an authentic human being. Ironically, this will strengthen your relationship with your children, and be a "win" in the parenting column. We all want our children to flourish, but altering reality will not help them succeed. Life isn't meant to be perfect. Sometimes you do well, other times you don't. The façade of happiness we display, whether it's in person or during our online activities, gives our kids a false sense of themselves. It sends a message that failing, making mistakes and being less than perfect is something shameful, something we hide and don't commend.

For example, if your kid does martial arts, you might be tempted to post something on Facebook about the fact that she just earned her next belt. While there's nothing wrong with a little bit of bragging, constant public displays of her achievements might be counterproductive. What about the one time she fails her belt test? Will you post her failure on Facebook as well? Will you tell your friends at the bus stop about it? Probably not, but going public only when things are perfect fosters the message: *I'm only proud of you when you achieve something.* We're not suggesting you post your failures all over the Internet, but is it really necessary to exaggerate how awesome your everyday reality really is?

We are at a time in history where we have the tools and ability to create any type of life we want. Why would we choose a mode of parenting that sets us up for isolation and failure? Instead let's use our social networks and the blogosphere to our advantage. Instead of focusing on your online village, put your efforts into building a *real* one using the technology available to us. Here are some suggestions to get started:

First, and most importantly, make the following pledge:

> *I, (insert your name here), pledge myself to the conscious unparenting™ movement. Instead of obsessing about all aspects of parenting, I'm going to "just do it," like those moms of the '70s. I will support my fellow moms both in person and online. I will prioritize my needs, acknowledging that, while my children's needs are important, they can no longer be the only ones that matter. By implementing these changes, I hope to experience more joy in parenting.*

Next, remember that disco ball we mentioned in the introduction? If you like what we're advocating, go to our website (*www.consciousunparenting.com*) and order a disco ball charm. Wear your charm on your wrist or neck, or dangle it from you purse or key chain – anywhere it can be seen and make a statement.

Displaying this symbol will hopefully accomplish several goals: (1) you're letting others know that you've taken the pledge, making a public statement that you're committed to a new mode of parenting; (2) you're telling other women that you're approachable, that safe harbor to whom you can say anything; and (3) you might make a new friend or two in your community. If nothing else, it's a conversation starter. ("Hey, you read that book by those dysfunctional moms from Rhode Island? Yeah, me too.")

Lastly, if you're serious about connecting with women locally, visit our website and we'll give you some tools for starting a discussion group in your area. These groups will be judgment-free zones; other than that, you can define the parameters. For example, Kim ran a group in San Diego that focused its emphasis on discipline and behavior strategies. The group met monthly at alternating homes. Each meeting, a group member presented a specific behavioral issue with which he or she was dealing. The rest of the group threw out suggestions based on their own experience and/or research. Respect for each other's opinions and parenting philosophies was given the utmost priority. Everyone had a chance to contribute and/or ask for advice.

You too can easily establish a similar group. To get you started, we've posted some suggestions on how to find and invite other parents, where to hold your meetings, structural guidelines and topics of discussion. Some examples include defining "success" for your children, how to deal with clutter and excess, and spousal/partner relationships.

We've all talked the talk about ending the mommy wars. It's time to walk the walk. We know this might be easier said than done. Taking a step back from your kids is terrifying. Making new friends is hard work. Publicly disavowing the entire notion of modern-day parenting might get you in trouble at the next PTA meeting. But we think it's worth the risk.

If you feel inspired by our stories, take a chance and make the pledge. You might experience the motherhood of your dreams, rather than the one of your nightmares. You can become a '70s mom with a 21st century twist. We've done it and we're experiencing more joy while parenting our children. Will you join us on our revolution to consciously unparent? Disco balls are a must; bell-bottoms and platform shoes – optional.

# ABOUT THE AUTHORS

***Kim Kinzie*** is a recovering attorney turned stay-at-home mom. After getting her BA at Bentley University, she headed to Law School. Having watched endless episodes of *Law and Order*, she decided to pursue a career as a prosecutor, hoping she'd have the opportunity to fight crime and work with cops who looked like Chris Noth. Though the latter part of that fantasy didn't pan out, she did dedicate her career to criminal law for the next eleven plus years. During that time she wrote the infamous *Massachusetts Prosecutors' Manual: Operating Under the Influence*. While not a *NY Times* bestseller, it did gain some cache in the local legal community. The process also helped Kim discover her true passion: writing. Since then she has dabbled in creative writing and has recently become a regular contributor for Rhode Island's *Motif Magazine*, where she writes profiles of local restaurants, festivals and kid-friendly activities. She now has her own column, *Alternative Parenting*, where she provides her unique perspective on child rearing. After years spent living in Boston and San Diego, she now resides in her home state of Rhode Island with her husband and their two boys.

***Dawn Michael*** graduated from Boston University with a degree in English and Biology. Though she would have loved to sustain a living by pondering Shakespeare, Dawn opted for the more lucrative and noble choice – optometry. After twenty years of asking the question, "Better one or two?" Dawn has decided to put her English degree to better use by writing a book. In addition to managing her optometric practice, Dawn provides a taxi service for her three ADHD children, shuttling them to their various play dates, recitals, and doctor's appointments. She spends the remainder of her free time battling with her husband that golf isn't the only means of exercise. Not one for change, Dawn currently resides in her native state of Rhode Island.